THE CHRISTIAN YEAR

THE

CHRISTIAN YEAR

THOUGHTS IN VERSE FOR
THE SUNDAYS AND HOLYDAYS
THROUGHOUT THE YEAR

*In quietness and in confidence shall
be your strength.*   Isaiah xxx, 15

By JOHN KEBLE

NEW YORK

D. APPLETON AND COMPANY

1896

Republished by Gale Research Company,
Book Tower, Detroit, 1975

Library of Congress Cataloging in Publication Data

Keble, John, 1792-1866.
  The Christian year.

  1. Church year–Poetry. I. Title.
PR4839.K15C4 1975.   821'.7   70-167019
ISBN 0-8103-4095-X

ADVERTISEMENT.

Next to a sound rule of faith, there is nothing of so
much consequence as a sober standard of feeling in
matters of practical religion : and it is the peculiar
happiness of the Church of England to possess, in her
authorized formularies, an ample and secure provision
for both. But in times of much leisure and unbounded
curiosity, when excitement of every kind is sought after
with a morbid eagerness, this part of the merit of our
Liturgy is likely in some measure to be lost, on many
even of its sincere admirers : the very tempers, which
most require such discipline, setting themselves, in
general, most decidedly against it.

The object of the present publication will be attained,
if any person find assistance from it in bringing his own
thoughts and feelings into more entire unison with those
recommended and exemplified in the Prayer Book. The
work does not furnish a complete series of compositions ;
being, in many parts, rather adapted with more or less
propriety to the successive portions of the Liturgy, than
originally suggested by them. Something has been added
at the end concerning the several Occasional Services :
which constitute, from their personal and domestic nature,
the most perfect instance of that *soothing* tendency in the
Prayer Book, which it is the chief purpose of these pages
to exhibit.

May 30th, 1827.

NOTE ON THE TEXT.

THE Third Edition of the CHRISTIAN YEAR, Oxford 1828, has served as the basis for the present text. It was the earliest complete edition, the first and second having ended with the poem on the Commination Service. It would also seem to be that which most exactly maintains Mr. Keble's own punctuation and spelling, variations in some later editions, mainly typographical, appearing to have no fixed principle.

The variations from the selected text are—α, the correction of a few obvious mis-prints; β, the Scriptural quotations have been restored to exact uniformity with the recognised version : these had been given with errors in punctuation and spelling, sometimes with alteration in words, though not in meaning, as if they had been written from memory; γ, the adoption from later editions of *oleanders* for *rhododendrons* in a note to the poem on the Third Sunday in Advent.

In the poem for Gunpowder Treason was made afterwards the only apparent doctrinal variation from the original work, but nothing need here be added to the controversy which the alteration aroused. It is enough to say that here, as elsewhere, the edition of 1828 is followed.

The etching has been taken by kind permission of Mr. George Richmond, R.A., from his well-known drawing of Mr. Keble, still in the artist's possession.

CONTENTS.

	PAGE
Morning	1
Evening	4
Advent Sunday	6
Second Sunday in Advent. *The Signs of the Times*	9
Third Sunday in Advent. *The Travellers*	11
Fourth Sunday in Advent. *Dimness*	14
Christmas Day	17
St. Stephen's Day	20
St. John's Day	22
The Holy Innocents	24
First Sunday after Christmas. *The Sun-dial of Ahaz*	26
The Circumcision	29
Second Sunday after Christmas. *The Pilgrim's Song*	32
The Epiphany	35
First Sunday after Epiphany. *The Nightingale*	38
Second Sunday after Epiphany. *The Secret of perpetual Youth*	40
Third Sunday after Epiphany. *The Good Centurion*	43
Fourth Sunday after Epiphany. *The World is for Excitement, the Gospel for Soothing*	46
Fifth Sunday after Epiphany. *Cure Sin and you cure Sorrow*	48
Sixth Sunday after Epiphany. *The Benefits of Uncertainty*	51
Septuagesima Sunday	54

	PAGE
Sexagesima Sunday	56
Quinquagesima Sunday	59
Ash-Wednesday	62
First Sunday in Lent. *The City of Refuge*	64
Second Sunday in Lent. *Esau's Forfeit*	66
Third Sunday in Lent. *The Spoils of Satan*	69
Fourth Sunday in Lent. *The Rose-bud*	71
Fifth Sunday in Lent. *The Burning Bush*	74
Sunday next before Easter. *The Children in the Temple* .	77
Monday before Easter. *Christ waiting for the Cross* . .	79
Tuesday before Easter. *Christ refusing the Wine and Myrrh*	82
Wednesday before Easter. *Christ in the Garden* . .	84
Thursday before Easter. *The Vision of the Latter Days* .	87
Good Friday	89
Easter Eve	91
Easter Day	94
Monday in Easter Week. *St. Peter and Cornelius* . .	97
Tuesday in Easter Week. *The Snow-drop* . . .	100
First Sunday after Easter. *The Restless Pastor reproved* .	103
Second Sunday after Easter. *Balaam*	106
Third Sunday after Easter. *Languor and Travail* . .	109
Fourth Sunday after Easter. *The Dove on the Cross* .	111
Fifth Sunday after Easter. *The Priest's Intercessor* . .	114
Ascension Day	117
Sunday after Ascension Day. *Seed time*	119
Whitsunday	122
Monday in Whitsun-week. *The City of Confusion* . .	124
Tuesday in Whitsun-week. *Holy Orders*	128
Trinity Sunday	131

PAGE

First Sunday after Trinity. *Israel among the Ruins of Canaan* 134

Second Sunday after Trinity. *Charity the Life of Faith* . 13ɔ

Third Sunday after Trinity. *Comfort for Sinners in the presence of the Good* 139

Fourth Sunday after Trinity. *The Groans of Nature* . . 141

Fifth Sunday after Trinity. *The Fishermen of Bethsaida* . 145

Sixth Sunday after Trinity. *The Psalmist repenting* . . 148

Seventh Sunday after Trinity. *The Feast in the Wilderness* 151

Eighth Sunday after Trinity. *The Disobedient Prophet* . 153

Ninth Sunday after Trinity. *Elijah in Horeb* . . . 155

Tenth Sunday after Trinity. *Christ weeping over Jerusalem* 158

Eleventh Sunday after Trinity. *Gehazi reproved* . . . 160

Twelfth Sunday after Trinity. *The Deaf and Dumb* . . 162

Thirteenth Sunday after Trinity. *Moses on the Mount* . . 165

Fourteenth Sunday after Trinity. *The Ten Lepers* . . 169

Fifteenth Sunday after Trinity. *The Flowers of the Field* . 171

Sixteenth Sunday after Trinity. *Hope is better than Ease* . 173

Seventeenth Sunday after Trinity. *Ezekiel's Vision in the Temple* 175

Eighteenth Sunday after Trinity. *The Church in the Wilderness* 178

Nineteenth Sunday after Trinity. *Shadrach, Meshach, and Abednego* 182

Twentieth Sunday after Trinity. *Mountain Scenery* . . 185

Twenty-first Sunday after Trinity. *The Red-breast in September* 187

Twenty-second Sunday after Trinity. *The Rule of Christian Forgiveness* 189

Twenty-third Sunday after Trinity. *Forest Leaves in Autumn* 191

Twenty-fourth Sunday after Trinity. *Imperfection of Human Sympathy* 194

PAGE

Twenty-fifth Sunday after Trinity. *The two Rainbows* . . 197

Sunday next before Advent. *Self-examination before Advent* 200

St. Andrew's Day 203

St. Thomas' 205

Conversion of St. Paul 208

Purification of St. Mary the Virgin 212

St. Matthias' Day 215

Annunciation of the Blessed Virgin Mary 217

St. Mark's Day 220

St. Philip and St. James's Day 222

St. Barnabas the Apostle 224

St. John Baptist's Day 227

St. Peter's Day 230

St. James the Apostle 233

St. Bartholomew the Apostle 235

St. Matthew the Apostle 238

St. Michael and all Angels 241

St. Luke the Evangelist 244

St. Simon and St. Jude, Apostles 248

All Saints' Day 250

Holy Communion 252

Holy Baptism 255

Catechism 257

Confirmation 259

Matrimony 261

Visitation and Communion of the Sick 263

Burial of the Dead 265

Churching of Women 268

Commination 270

	PAGE
Forms of Prayer to be used at Sea	272
Gunpowder Treason	274
King Charles the Martyr	277
The Restoration of the Royal Family	279
The Accession	281
Ordination	283
Index	285

THE CHRISTIAN YEAR.

Morning. *His compassions fail not. They are new every morning.* Lament. iii. 22, 23.

H UES of the rich unfolding morn,
　　That, ere the glorious sun be born,
By some soft touch invisible
Around his path are taught to swell ;—

Thou rustling breeze so fresh and gay,
That dancest forth at opening day,
And brushing by with joyous wing,
Wakenest each little leaf to sing ;—

Ye fragrant clouds of dewy steam,
By which deep grove and tangled stream
Pay, for soft rains in season given,
Their tribute to the genial heaven ;—

Why waste your treasures of delight
Upon our thankless, joyless sight ;
Who day by day to sin awake,
Seldom of heaven and you partake ?

Oh ! timely happy, timely wise,
Hearts that with rising morn arise !
Eyes that the beam celestial view,
Which evermore makes all things new [a].

[a] Revelation xxi. 5.

New every morning is the love
Our wakening and uprising prove ;
Through sleep and darkness safely brought,
Restored to life, and power, and thought.

New mercies, each returning day,
Hover around us while we pray ;
New perils past, new sins forgiven,
New thoughts of God, new hopes of heaven.

If on our daily course our mind
Be set to hallow all we find,
New treasures still, of countless price,
God will provide for sacrifice.

Old friends, old scenes, will lovelier be,
As more of heaven in each we see :
Some softening gleam of love and prayer
Shall dawn on every cross and care.

As for some dear familiar strain
Untir'd we ask, and ask again,
Ever, in its melodious store,
Finding a spell unheard before ;

Such is the bliss of souls serene,
When they have sworn, and stedfast mean,
Counting the cost, in all to espy
Their God, in all themselves deny.

O could we learn that sacrifice,
What lights would all around us rise !
How would our hearts with wisdom talk
Along Life's dullest dreariest walk !

We need not bid, for cloister'd cell,
Our neighbour and our work farewell,
Nor strive to wind ourselves too high
For sinful man beneath the sky :

The trivial round, the common task,
Would furnish all we ought to ask ;
Room to deny ourselves ; a road
To bring us, daily, nearer God.

Seek we no more ; content with these,
Let present Rapture, Comfort, Ease,
As Heaven shall bid them, come and go :—
The secret this of Rest below.

Only, O Lord, in thy dear love
Fit us for perfect Rest above ;
And help us, this and every day,
To live more nearly as we pray.

Evening.

Abide with us : for it is toward evening, and the day is far spent. St. Luke xxiv. 29.

'TIS gone, that bright and orbed blaze,
　Fast fading from our wistful gaze ;
Yon mantling cloud has hid from sight
The last faint pulse of quivering light.

In darkness and in weariness
The traveller on his way must press,
No gleam to watch on tree or tower,
Whiling away the lonesome hour.

Sun of my soul ! Thou Saviour dear,
It is not night if Thou be near :
Oh may no earth-born cloud arise
To hide Thee from thy servant's eyes.

When round thy wondrous works below
My searching rapturous glance I throw,
Tracing out Wisdom, Power, and Love,
In earth or sky, in stream or grove ;—

Or by the light thy words disclose
Watch Time's full river as it flows,
Scanning thy gracious Providence,
Where not too deep for mortal sense :—

When with dear friends sweet talk I hold,
And all the flowers of life unfold ;—
Let not my heart within me burn,
Except in all I Thee discern.

When the soft dews of kindly sleep
My wearied eyelids gently steep,

Be my last thought, how sweet to rest
For ever on my Saviour's breast.

Abide with me from morn till eve,
For without Thee I cannot live :
Abide with me when night is nigh,
For without Thee I dare not die.

Thou Framer of the light and dark,
Steer through the tempest thine own ark :
Amid the howling wintry sea
We are in port if we have Thee b.

The Rulers of this Christian land,
'Twixt Thee and us ordained to stand,—
Guide Thou their course, O Lord, aright,
Let all do all as in thy sight.

Oh by thine own sad burthen, borne
So meekly up the hill of scorn,
Teach Thou thy Priests their daily cross
To bear as thine, nor count it loss !

If some poor wandering child of thine
Have spurn'd, to-day, the voice divine,
Now, Lord, the gracious work begin ;
Let him no more lie down in sin.

Watch by the sick : enrich the poor
With blessings from thy boundless store :
Be every mourner's sleep to-night
Like infants' slumbers, pure and light.

Come near and bless us when we wake,
Ere through the world our way we take :
Till in the ocean of thy love
We lose ourselves in heaven above.

b Then they willingly received him into the ship . and immediately the ship was at the land whither they went. *St. John*
vi. 21.

Advent Sunday.

Now it is high time to awake out of sleep: for now is our salvation nearer than when we believed. Romans xiii. 11.

AWAKE—again the Gospel-trump is blown—
From year to year it swells with louder tone,
From year to year the signs of wrath
Are gathering round the Judge's path,
Strange words fulfill'd, and mighty works achiev'd,
And truth in all the world both hated and believ'd.

Awake! why linger in the gorgeous town,
Sworn liegemen of the Cross and thorny crown?
Up from your beds of sloth for shame,
Speed to the eastern mount like flame,
Nor wonder, should ye find your King in tears,
Even with the loud Hosanna ringing in his ears.

Alas! no need to rouse them : long ago
They are gone forth, to swell Messiah's show :
With glittering robes and garlands sweet
They strew the ground beneath his feet :
All but your hearts are there—O doom'd to prove
The arrows wing'd in Heaven for Faith that will not love!

Meanwhile He paces through th' adoring crowd,
Calm as the march of some majestic cloud,
That o'er wild scenes of ocean-war
Holds its still course in heaven afar :
Even so, heart-searching Lord, as years roll on,
Thou keepest silent watch from thy triumphal throne :

Even so, the world is thronging round to gaze
On the dread vision of the latter days,
    Constrain'd to own Thee, but in heart
    Prepared to take Barabbas' part :
" Hosanna " now, to-morrow " Crucify,"
The changeful burden still of their rude lawless cry.

Yet in that throng of selfish hearts untrue
Thy sad eye rests upon thy faithful few,
    Children and childlike souls are there,
    Blind Bartimeus' humble prayer,
And Lazarus waken'd from his four days' sleep,
Enduring life again, that Passover to keep.

And fast beside the olive-border'd way
Stands the bless'd home, where Jesus deign'd to stay,
    The peaceful home, to Zeal sincere
    And heavenly Contemplation dear,
Where Martha lov'd to wait with reverence meet,
And wiser Mary linger'd at thy sacred feet.

Still through decaying ages as they glide,
Thou lov'st thy chosen remnant to divide ;
    Sprinkled along the waste of years
    Full many a soft green isle appears :
Pause where we may upon the desert road,
Some shelter is in sight, some sacred safe abode.

When withering blasts of error swept the sky [c],
And Love's last flower seem'd fain to droop and die,
    How sweet, how lone the ray benign
    On shelter'd nooks of Palestine !
Then to his early home did Love repair [d],
And cheer'd his sickening heart with his own native air.

[c] Arianism in the fourth century.
[d] See St. Jerome's Works, i. 123, edit. Erasm.

Years roll away : again the tide of crime
Has swept thy footsteps from the favour'd clime.
    Where shall the holy Cross find rest?
    On a crown'd monarch's e mailed breast :
Like some bright angel o'er the darkling scene,
Through court and camp he holds his heavenward course
    serene.

A fouler vision yet ; an age of light,
Light without love, glares on the aching sight :
    O who can tell how calm and sweet,
    Meek Walton ! shews thy green retreat,
When wearied with the tale thy times disclose,
The eye first finds thee out in thy secure repose?

Thus bad and good their several warnings give
Of His approach, whom none may see and live :
    Faith's ear, with awful still delight,
    Counts them like minute-bells at night,
Keeping the heart awake till dawn of morn,
While to her funeral pile this aged world is borne.

But what are heaven's alarms to hearts that cower
In wilful slumber, deepening every hour,
    That draw their curtains closer round,
    The nearer swells the trumpet's sound !
Lord, ere our trembling lamps sink down and die,
Touch us with chastening hand, and make us feel Thee
    nigh.

    e St. Louis in the thirteenth century.

Second Sunday in Advent.

And when these things begin to come to pass, then look up, and lift up your heads; for your redemption draweth nigh. St. Luke xxi. 28.

NOT till the freezing blast is still,
　　Till freely leaps the sparkling rill,
And gales sweep soft from summer skies,
As o'er a sleeping infant's eyes
A mother's kiss; ere calls like these,
No sunny gleam awakes the trees,
Nor dare the tender flowerets show
Their bosoms to th' uncertain glow.

Why then, in sad and wintry time,
Her heavens all dark with doubt and crime,
Why lifts the Church her drooping head,
As though her evil hour were fled?
Is she less wise than leaves of spring,
Or birds that cower with folded wing?
What sees she in this lowering sky
To tempt her meditative eye?

She has a charm, a word of fire,
A pledge of love that cannot tire;
By tempests, earthquakes, and by wars,
By rushing waves and falling stars,
By every sign her Lord foretold,
She sees the world is waxing old f,
And through that last and direst storm
Descries by faith her Saviour's form.

f The world hath lost his youth, and the times begin to wax old. 2 *Esdras* xiv. 10.

Not surer does each tender gem,
Set in the fig tree's polish'd stem,
Foreshew the summer season bland,
Than these dread signs thy mighty hand :
But oh ! frail hearts, and spirits dark !
The season's flight unwarn'd we mark,
But miss the Judge behind the door g,
For all the light of sacred lore :

Yet is He there : beneath our eaves
Each sound his wakeful ear receives :
Hush, idle words, and thoughts of ill,
Your Lord is listening : peace, be still h.
Christ watches by a Christian's hearth,
Be silent, " vain deluding mirth,"
Till in thine alter'd voice be known
Somewhat of Resignation's tone.

But chiefly ye should lift your gaze
Above the world's uncertain haze,
And look with calm unwavering eye
On the bright fields beyond the sky,
Ye, who your Lord's commission bear,
His way of mercy to prepare :
Angels He calls ye : be your strife
To lead on earth an Angel's life.

Think not of rest ; though dreams be sweet,
Start up, and ply your heaven-ward feet.
Is not God's oath upon your head,
Ne'er to sink back on slothful bed,
Never again your loins untie,
Nor let your torches waste and die,
Till, when the shadows thickest fall,
Ye hear your Master's midnight call ?

g See St. James v. 9.
  h Ita fabulantur, ut qui sciant Dominum audire. *Tertull.*
Apolog. p. 36, edit. Rigalt.

Third Sunday in Advent.

What went ye out into the wilderness to see? A reed shaken with the wind?... But what went ye out for to see? a prophet? yea, I say unto you, and more than a prophet. St. Matthew xi. 7, 9.

WHAT went ye out to see
 O'er the rude sandy lea,
Where stately Jordan flows by many a palm,
 Or where Gennesaret's wave
 Delights the flowers to lave,
That o'er her western slope breathe airs of balm?

 All through the summer night,
 Those blossoms red and bright [1]
Spread their soft breasts, unheeding, to the breeze,
 Like hermits watching still
 Around the sacred hill,
Where erst our Saviour watch'd upon his knees.

 The Paschal moon above
 Seems like a saint to rove,
Left shining in the world with Christ alone;
 Below, the lake's still face
 Sleeps sweetly in th' embrace
Of mountains terrac'd high with mossy stone.

 Here may we sit, and dream
 Over the heavenly theme,
Till to our soul the former days return;

[1] Oleanders: with which the western bank of the lake is said to be clothed down to the water's edge.

Till on the grassy bed,
Where thousands once He fed,
The world's incarnate Maker we discern.

O cross no more the main,
Wandering so wild and vain,
To count the reeds that tremble in the wind,
On listless dalliance bound,
Like children gazing round,
Who on God's works no seal of Godhead find :

Bask not in courtly bower,
Or sun-bright hall of power,
Pass Babel quick, and seek the holy land—
From robes of Tyrian die
Turn with undazzled eye
To Bethlehem's glade, or Carmel's haunted strand.

Or choose thee out a cell
In Kedron's storied dell,
Beside the springs of Love, that never die,
Among the olives kneel
The chill night-blast to feel,
And watch the Moon that saw thy Master's agony.

Then rise at dawn of day,
And wind thy thoughtful way,
Where rested once the Temple's stately shade,
With due feet tracing round
The city's northern bound,
To th' other holy garden, where the Lord was laid.

Who thus alternate see
His death and victory,
Rising and falling as on angel wings,
They, while they seem to roam,
Draw daily nearer home,
Their heart untravell'd still adores the King of kings.

Or, if at home they stay,
Yet are they, day by day,
In spirit journeying through the glorious land,
Not for light Fancy's reed,
Nor Honour's purple meed,
Nor gifted Prophet's lore, nor Science' wondrous wand.

But more than Prophet, more
Than Angels can adore
With face unveil'd, is He they go to seek :
Blessed be God, whose grace
Shews Him in every place
To homeliest hearts of pilgrims pure and meek.

Fourth Sunday in Advent.

The eyes of them that see shall not be dim, and the ears of them that hear shall hearken. Isaiah xxxii. 3.

OF the bright things in earth and air
　　How little can the heart embrace !
Soft shades and gleaming lights are there—
　　I know it well, but cannot trace.

Mine eye unworthy seems to read
　　One page of Nature's beauteous book ;
It lies before me, fair outspread—
　　I only cast a wishful look.

I cannot paint to Memory's eye
　　The scene, the glance, I dearest love—
Unchang'd themselves, in me they die,
　　Or faint, or false, their shadows prove.

In vain, with dull and tuneless ear,
　　I linger by soft Music's cell,
And in my heart of hearts would hear
　　What to her own she deigns to tell.

'Tis misty all, both sight and sound—
　　I only know 'tis fair and sweet—
'Tis wandering on enchanted ground
　　With dizzy brow and tottering feet.

But patience ! there may come a time
　　When these dull ears shall scan aright
Strains, that outring Earth's drowsy chime,
　　As Heaven outshines the taper's light.

These eyes, that dazzled now and weak,
  At glancing motes in sunshine wink,
Shall see the King's ⃰ full glory break,
  Nor from the blissful vision shrink :

In fearless love and hope uncloy'd
  For ever on that ocean bright
Empower'd to gaze ; and undestroy'd,
  Deeper and deeper plunge in light.

Though scarcely now their laggard glance
  Reach to an arrow's flight, that day
They shall behold, and not in trance,
  The region " very far away."

If Memory sometimes at our spell
  Refuse to speak, or speak amiss,
We shall not need her where we dwell
  Ever in sight of all our bliss.

Meanwhile, if over sea or sky
  Some tender lights unnotic'd fleet,
Or on lov'd features dawn and die,
  Unread, to us, their lesson sweet ;

Yet are there saddening sights around,
  Which Heaven, in mercy, spares us too,
And we see far in holy ground,
  If duly purg'd our mental view.

The distant landscape draws not nigh
  For all our gazing ; but the soul,
That upward looks, may still descry
  Nearer, each day, the brightening goal.

⃰ Thine eyes shall see the king in his beauty : they shall behold
the land that is very far off. *Isaiah* xxxiii. 17.

And thou, too curious ear, that fain
    Wouldst thread the maze of Harmony,
Content thee with one simple strain,
    The lowlier, sure, the worthier thee ;

Till thou art duly trained, and taught
    The concord sweet of Love divine :
Then, with that inward Music fraught
    For ever rise, and sing, and shine.

Christmas Day.

And suddenly there was with the angel a multitude of the heavenly host praising God. St. Luke ii. 13.

W HAT sudden blaze of song
  Spreads o'er th' expanse of Heav'n?
In waves of light it thrills along,
  Th' angelic signal given—
"Glory to God!" from yonder central fire
Flows out the echoing lay beyond the starry quire ;

  Like circles widening round
    Upon a clear blue river,
  Orb after orb, the wondrous sound
    Is echoed on for ever :
"Glory to God on high, on earth be peace,
And love towards men of love k—salvation and release."

  Yet stay, before thou dare
    To join that festal throng ;
  Listen and mark what gentle air
    First stirr'd the tide of song ;
'Tis not, " the Saviour born in David's home,
" To whom for power and health obedient worlds should
    come :"—

  'Tis not, "the Christ the Lord :"—
    With fix'd adoring look

---

k I have ventured to adopt the reading of the Vulgate, as being generally known through Pergolesi's beautiful composition "Gloria in excelsis Deo, et in terra pax *hominibus bonæ voluntatis.*'

3

The choir of Angels caught the word,
    Nor yet their silence broke :
But when they heard the sign, where Christ should be,
In sudden light they shone and heavenly harmony.

    Wrapp'd in his swaddling bands,
      And in his manger laid,
    The hope and glory of all lands
      Is come to the world's aid :
No peaceful home upon his cradle smil'd,
Guests rudely went and came, where slept the royal child.

    But where Thou dwellest, Lord,
      No other thought should be,
    Once duly welcom'd and ador'd,
      How should I part with Thee ?
Bethlehem must lose Thee soon, but Thou wilt grace
The single heart to be thy sure abiding-place.

    Thee, on the bosom laid
      Of a pure virgin mind,
    In quiet ever, and in shade,
      Shepherd and sage may find ;
They, who have bow'd untaught to Nature's sway,
And they, who follow Truth along her star-pav'd way.

    The pastoral spirits first
      Approach Thee, Babe divine,
    For they in lowly thoughts are nurs'd,
      Meet for thy lowly shrine :
Sooner than they should miss where Thou dost dwell,
Angels from Heaven will stoop to guide them to thy cell.

    Still, as the day comes round
      For Thee to be reveal'd,
    By wakeful shepherds Thou art found,
      Abiding in the field.

All through the wintry heaven and chill night air,
In music and in light Thou dawnest on their prayer.

O faint not ye for fear—
What though your wandering sheep,
Reckless of what they see and hear,
Lie lost in wilful sleep?
High Heaven in mercy to your sad annoy
Still greets you with glad tidings of immortal joy.

Think on th' eternal home,
The Saviour left for you ;
Think on the Lord most holy, come
To dwell with hearts untrue :
So shall ye tread untir'd his pastoral ways,
And in the darkness sing your carol of high praise.

St. Stephen's Day.

He, being full of the Holy Ghost, looked up stedfastly into heaven, and saw the glory of God, and Jesus standing on the right hand of God. Acts vii. 55.

A S rays around the source of light
    Stream upward ere he glow in sight,
And watching by his future flight
    Set the clear heavens on fire ;
So on the King of Martyrs wait
Three chosen bands, in royal state [1],
And all earth owns, of good and great
    Is gather'd in that choir.

One presses on, and welcomes death :
One calmly yields his willing breath,
Nor slow, nor hurrying, but in faith
    Content to die or live :
And some, the darlings of their Lord,
Play smiling with the flame and sword,
And, ere they speak, to his sure word
    Unconscious witness give.

Foremost and nearest to his throne,
By perfect robes of triumph known,

[1] Wheatley no the Common Prayer, c. v. sect. iv. 2. "As there are three kinds of martyrdom, the first both in will and deed, which is the highest ; the second in will but not in deed ; the third in deed but not in will ; so the Church commemorates these martyrs in the same order : St. Stephen first, who suffered death both in will and deed ; St. John the Evangelist next, who suffered martyrdom in will but not in deed ; the holy Innocents last, who suffered in deed but not in will."

And likest Him in look and tone,
    The holy Stephen kneels,
With stedfast gaze, as when the sky
Flew open to his fainting eye,
Which, like a fading lamp, flash'd high,
    Seeing what death conceals.

Well might you guess what vision bright
Was present to his raptur'd sight,
Even as reflected streams of light
    Their solar source betray—
The glory which our God surrounds,
The Son of Man, th' atoning wounds—
He sees them all ; and earth's dull bounds
    Are melting fast away.

He sees them all—no other view
Could stamp the Saviour's likeness true,
Or with his love so deep embrue
    Man's sullen heart and gross—
"Jesu, do Thou my soul receive :
"Jesu, do Thou my foes forgive :"
He who would learn that prayer, must live
    Under the holy Cross.

He, though he seem on earth to move,
Must glide in air like gentle dove,
From yon unclouded depths above
    Must draw his purer breath ;
Till men behold his angel face
All radiant with celestial grace [m],
Martyr all o'er, and meet to trace
    The lines of Jesus' death.

[m] And all that sat in the council, looking stedfastly on him, saw his face as it had been the face of an angel. *Acts* vi. 15.

St. John's Day.

Peter seeing him saith to Jesus, Lord, and what shall this man do? Jesus saith unto him, If I will that he tarry till I come, what is that to thee? follow thou me. St. John xxi. 21, 22

" LORD, and what shall this man do? "
    Ask'st thou, Christian, for thy friend?
If his love for Christ be true,
    Christ hath told thee of his end :
This is he whom God approves,
This is he whom Jesus loves.

Ask not of Him more than this,
    Leave it in his Saviour's breast,
Whether, early call'd to bliss,
    He in youth shall find his rest,
Or armed in his station wait
Till his Lord be at the gate :

Whether in his lonely course,
    Lonely, not forlorn, he stay,
Or with Love's supporting force
    Cheat the toil and cheer the way :
Leave it all in His high hand,
Who doth hearts as streams command [n].

Gales from heaven, if so He will,
    Sweeter melodies can wake
On the lonely mountain rill
    Than the meeting waters make.

[n] The king's heart is in the hand of the Lord, as the rivers of water : he turneth it whithersoever he will. *Proverbs* xxi. 1.

Who hath the Father and the Son,
May be left, but not alone.

Sick or healthful, slave or free,
    Wealthy, or despis'd and poor—
What is that to him or thee,
    So his love to Christ endure?
When the shore is won at last,
Who will count the billows past?

Only, since our souls will shrink
    At the touch of natural grief,
When our earthly lov'd ones sink,
    Lend us, Lord, thy sure relief;
Patient hearts, their pain to see,
And thy grace, to follow Thee.

The Holy Innocents

These were redeemed from among men, being the firstfruits unto God and to the Lamb.
Rev. xiv. 4.

SAY, ye celestial guards, who wait
   In Bethlehem, round the Saviour's palace gate,
Say, who are these on golden wings,
That hover o'er the new-born King of kings,
   Their palms and garlands telling plain
That they are of the glorious martyr train,
   Next to yourselves ordain'd to praise
His name, and brighten as on Him they gaze?

But where their spoils and trophies? where
The glorious dint a martyr's shield should bear?
   How chance no cheek among them wears
The deep-worn trace of penitential tears,
   But all is bright and smiling love,
As if, fresh-borne from Eden's happy grove,
   They had flown here, their King to see,
Nor ever had been heirs of dark mortality?

   Ask, and some angel will reply,
" These, like yourselves, were born to sin and die,
   " But ere the poison root was grown,
" God set his seal, and mark'd them for his own.
   " Baptiz'd in blood for Jesus' sake,
" Now underneath the cross their bed they make,
   " Not to be scar'd from that sure rest
" By frighten'd mother's shriek, or warrior's waving crest."

Mindful of these, the first-fruits sweet
Borne by the suffering Church her Lord to greet ;
   Bless'd Jesus ever lov'd to trace
The "innocent brightness" of an infant's face.
   He rais'd them in his holy arms,
He bless'd them from the world and all its harms :
   Heirs though they were of sin and shame,
He bless'd them in his own and in his Father's name.

   Then, as each fond unconscious child
On th' everlasting Parent sweetly smil'd,
   Like infants sporting on the shore,
That tremble not at Ocean's boundless roar,
   Were they not present to thy thought,
All souls, that in their cradles thou hast bought ?
   But chiefly these, who died for Thee,
That Thou might'st live for them a sadder death to see.

   And next to these, thy gracious word
Was as a pledge of benediction, stor'd
   For Christian mothers, while they moan
Their treasur'd hopes, just born, baptiz'd, and gone.
   Oh joy for Rachel's broken heart !
She and her babes shall meet no more to part ;
   So dear to Christ her pious haste
To trust them in his arms, for ever safe embrac'd.

   She dares not grudge to leave them there,
Where to behold them was her heart's first prayer,
   She dares not grieve—but she must weep,
As her pale placid martyr sinks to sleep,
   Teaching so well and silently
How, at the shepherd's call, the lamb should die :
   How happier far than life the end
Of souls that infant-like beneath their burthen bend.

First Sunday after Christmas.

So the sun returned ten degrees, by which degrees it was gone down. Isaiah xxxviii. 8; compare Joshua x. 13.

'TIS true, of old th' unchanging sun
    His daily course refus'd to run,
      The pale moon hurrying to the west
    Paus'd at a mortal's call, to aid
    Th' avenging storm of war, that laid
Seven guilty realms at once on earth's defiled breast.

    But can it be, one suppliant tear
    Should stay the ever-moving sphere?
      A sick man's lowly breathed sigh,
    When from the world he turns away °,
    And hides his weary eyes to pray,
Should change your mystic dance, ye wanderers of the
      sky?

    We too, O Lord, would fain command,
    As then, thy wonder-working hand,
      And backward force the waves of Time,
    That now so swift and silent bear
    Our restless bark from year to year;
Help us to pause and mourn to Thee our tale of crime.

    Bright hopes, that erst the bosom warm'd,
    And vows, too pure to be perform'd,
      And prayers blown wide by gales of care;—

° Then Hezekiah turned his face toward the wall, and prayed unto the Lord. *Isaiah* xxxviii. 2.

These, and such faint half waking dreams,
Like stormy lights on mountain streams,
Wavering and broken all, athwart the conscience glare.

How shall we 'scape th' o'erwhelming Past?
Can spirits broken, joys o'ercast,
  And eyes that never more may smile :—
Can these th' avenging bolt delay,
Or win us back one little day
The bitterness of death to soften and beguile?

Father and Lover of our souls!
Though darkly round thine anger rolls,
  Thy sunshine smiles beneath the gloom,
Thou seek'st to warn us, not confound,
Thy showers would pierce the harden'd ground,
.And win it to give out its brightness and perfume.

Thou smil'st on us in wrath, and we,
Even in remorse, would smile on Thee ;
  The tears that bathe our offer'd hearts,
We would not have them stain'd and dim,
But dropp'd from wings of seraphim,
All glowing with the light accepted Love imparts.

Time's waters will not ebb, nor stay,
Power cannot change them, but Love may ;
  What cannot be, Love counts it done.
Deep in the heart, her searching view
Can read where Faith is fix'd and true,
Through shades of setting life can see Heaven's work
      begun.

O Thou, who keep'st the Key of Love,
Open thy fount, eternal Dove,
  And overflow this heart of mine,

Enlarging as it fills with Thee,
Till in one blaze of charity
Care and remorse are lost, like motes in light divine ;

Till, as each moment wafts us higher,
By every gush of pure desire,
    And high-breath'd hope of joys above,
By every sacred sigh we heave,
Whole years of folly we outlive,
In His unerring sight, who measures Life by Love.

The Circumcision of Christ.

In whom also ye are circumcised with the circumcision made without hands. Coloss. ii. 11.

THE year begins with Thee,
    And Thou beginn'st with woe,
To let the world of sinners see
    That blood for sin must flow.

Thine infant cries, O Lord,
    Thy tears upon the breast,
Are not enough—the legal sword
    Must do its stern behest.

Like sacrificial wine
    Pour'd on a victim's head
Are those few precious drops of thine,
    Now first to offering led.

They are the pledge and seal
    Of Christ's unswerving faith
Given to his Sire, our souls to heal,
    Although it cost his death.

They to his church of old,
    To each true Jewish heart,
In Gospel graces manifold
    Communion blest impart.

Now of thy love we deem
    As of an ocean vast,
Mounting in tides against the stream
    Of ages gone and past.

Both theirs and ours Thou art,
  As we and they are thine ;
Kings, Prophets, Patriarchs—all have part
  Along the sacred line.

By blood and water too
  God's mark is set on Thee,
That in Thee every faithful view
  Both covenants might see.

O bond of union, dear
  And strong as is Thy grace !
Saints, parted by a thousand year,
  May thus in heart embrace.

Is there a mourner true,
  Who fallen on faithless days,
Sighs for the heart-consoling view
  Of those, Heaven deign'd to praise ?

In spirit may'st thou meet
  With faithful Abraham here,
Whom soon in Eden thou shalt greet
  A nursing Father dear.

Wouldst thou a Poet be ?
  And would thy dull heart fain
Borrow of Israel's minstrelsy
  One high enraptur'd strain ?

Come here thy soul to tune,
  Here set thy feeble chant,
Here, if at all beneath the moon,
  Is holy David's haunt.

Art thou a child of tears,
  Cradled in care and woe ?
And seems it hard, thy vernal years
  Few vernal joys can shew ?

And fall the sounds of mirth
Sad on thy lonely heart,
From all the hopes and charms of earth
Untimely call'd to part?

Look here, and hold thy peace :
The Giver of all good
Even from the womb takes no release
From suffering, tears, and blood.

If thou wouldst reap in love,
First sow in holy fear :
So life a winter's morn may prove
To a bright endless year.

Second Sunday after Christmas.

When the poor and needy seek water, and there is none, and their tongue faileth for thirst, I the Lord will hear them, I the God of Israel will not forsake them. Isaiah xli. 17.

AND wilt Thou hear the fever'd heart
　　To Thee in silence cry?
And as th' inconstant wildfires dart
　　Out of the restless eye,
Wilt Thou forgive the wayward thought,
By kindly woes yet half untaught
A Saviour's right, so dearly bought,
　　That Hope should never die?

Thou wilt : for many a languid prayer
　　Has reach'd Thee from the wild,
Since the lorn mother, wandering there,
　　Cast down her fainting child P,
Then stole apart to weep and die,
Nor knew an angel form was nigh
To shew soft waters gushing by
　　And dewy shadows mild.

Thou wilt—for Thou art Israel's God,
　　And thine unwearied arm
Is ready yet with Moses' rod,
　　The hidden rill to charm
Out of the dry unfathom'd deep
Of sands, that lie in lifeless sleep,
Save when the scorching whirlwinds heap
　　Their waves in rude alarm.

　　　P Hagar. See Genesis xxi. 15.

Those moments of wild wrath are thine—
    Thine too the drearier hour
When o'er th' horizon's silent line
    Fond hopeless fancies cower,
And on the traveller's listless way
Rises and sets th' unchanging day,
No cloud in heaven to slake its ray,
    On earth no sheltering bower.

Thou wilt be there, and not forsake,
    To turn the bitter pool
Into a bright and breezy lake,
    The throbbing brow to cool :
Till left awhile with Thee alone
The wilful heart be fain to own
That He, by whom our bright hours shone,
    Our darkness best may rule.

The scent of water far away
    Upon the breeze is flung :
The desert pelican to-day
    Securely leaves her young,
Reproving thankless man, who fears
To journey on a few lone years,
Where on the sand thy step appears,
    Thy crown in sight is hung.

Thou, who didst sit on Jacob's well
    The weary hour of noon [q],
The languid pulses Thou canst tell,
    The nerveless spirit tune.
Thou from whose cross in anguish burst
The cry that own'd thy dying thirst [r],
To Thee we turn, our last and first,
    Our Sun and soothing Moon.

[q] St. John iv. 6.   [r] St. John xix. 28.

4

From darkness, here, and dreariness
    We ask not full repose,
Only be Thou at hand, to bless
    Our trial hour of woes.
Is not the pilgrim's toil o'erpaid
By the clear rill and palmy shade?
And see we not, up Earth's dark glade,
    The gate of Heaven unclose?

The Epiphany.

And, lo, the star, which they saw in the east, went before them, till it came and stood over where the young child was. When they saw the star, they rejoiced with exceeding great joy.
St. Matthew ii. 9, 10.

STAR of the East, how sweet art Thou,
　　Seen in Life's early morning sky,
Ere yet a cloud has dimm'd the brow,
　　While yet we gaze with childish eye;

When father, mother, nursing friend,
　　Most dearly lov'd, and loving best,
First bid us from their arms ascend,
　　Pointing to Thee in thy sure rest.

Too soon the glare of earthly day
　　Buries, to us, thy brightness keen,
And we are left to find our way
　　By faith and hope in Thee unseen.

What matter? if the waymarks sure
　　On every side are round us set,
Soon overleap'd, but not obscure?
　　'Tis ours to mark them or forget.

What matter? if in calm old age
　　Our childhood's star again arise,
Crowning our lonely pilgrimage
　　With all that cheers a wanderer's eyes?

Ne'er may we lose it from our sight,
  Till all our hopes and thoughts are led
To where it stays its lucid flight
  Over our Saviour's lowly bed.

There, swath'd in humblest poverty,
  On Chastity's meek lap enshrin'd,
With breathless Reverence waiting by,
  When we our sovereign Master find.

Will not the long-forgotten glow
  Of mingled joy and awe return,
When stars above or flowers below
  First made our infant spirits burn?

Look on us, Lord, and take our parts
  Even on thy throne of purity!
From these our proud yet grovelling hearts
  Hide not thy mild forgiving eye.

Did not the Gentile Church find grace,
  Our mother dear, this favour'd day?
With gold and myrrh she sought thy face,
  Nor didst Thou turn thy face away.

She too [s], in earlier, purer days,
  Had watch'd Thee gleaming faint and far—
But wandering in self-chosen ways
  She lost Thee quite, thou lovely star.

Yet had her Father's finger turn'd
  To Thee her first enquiring glance:
The deeper shame within her burn'd,
  When waken'd from her wilful trance.

[s] The Patriarchal Church.

Behold, her wisest throng thy gate,
    Their richest, sweetest, purest store,
Yet own'd too worthless and too late,
    They lavish on Thy cottage-floor.

They give their best—O tenfold shame
    On us their fallen progeny,
Who sacrifice the blind and lame[t]—
    Who will not wake or fast with Thee !

[t] Malachi i. 8.

First Sunday after Epiphany.

They shall spring up as among the grass, as willows by the water courses.— Isaiah xliv. 4.

L ESSONS sweet of spring returning,
    Welcome to the thoughtful heart !
May I call you sense or learning,
    Instinct pure, or heav'n-taught art ?
Be your title what it may,
Sweet the lengthening April day,
While with you the soul is free,
Ranging wild o'er hill and lea.

Soft as Memnon's harp at morning,
    To the inward ear devout,
Touch'd by light, with heavenly warning
    Your transporting chords ring out.
Every leaf in every nook,
Every wave in every brook,
Chanting with a solemn voice,
Minds us of our better choice.

Needs no show of mountain hoary,
    Winding shore or deepening glen,
Where the landscape in its glory
    Teaches truth to wandering men :
Give true hearts but earth and sky,
And some flowers to bloom and die,—
Homely scenes and simple views
Lowly thoughts may best infuse.

See the soft green willow springing
    Where the waters gently pass,

Every way her free arms flinging
  O'er the moist and reedy grass.
Long ere winter blasts are fled,
See her tipp'd with vernal red,
And her kindly flower display'd
Ere her leaf can cast a shade.

Though the rudest hand assail her,
  Patiently she droops awhile,
But when showers and breezes hail her,
  Wears again her willing smile.
Thus I learn Contentment's power
From the slighted willow bower,
Ready to give thanks and live
On the least that Heaven may give.

If, the quiet brooklet leaving,
  Up the stony vale I wind,
Haply half in fancy grieving
  For the shades I leave behind,
By the dusty wayside drear,
Nightingales with joyous cheer
Sing, my sadness to reprove,
Gladlier than in cultur'd grove.

Where the thickest boughs are twining
  Of the greenest darkest tree,
There they plunge, the light declining—
  All may hear, but none may see.
Fearless of the passing hoof,
Hardly will they fleet aloof;
So they live in modest ways,
Trust entire, and ceaseless praise.

Second Sunday after Epiphany.

Every man at the beginning doth set forth good wine; and when men have well drunk, then that which is worse : but thou hast kept the good wine until now.
St. John ii. 10.

T HE heart of childhood is all mirth :
    We frolic to and fro
As free and blithe, as if on earth
    Were no such thing as woe.

But if indeed with reckless faith
    We trust the flattering voice,
Which whispers, " Take thy fill ere death,
    " Indulge thee and rejoice ;"

Too surely, every setting day,
    Some lost delight we mourn,
The flowers all die along our way,
    Till we, too, die forlorn.

Such is the world's gay garish feast,
    In her first charming bowl
Infusing all that fires the breast,
    And cheats th' unstable soul.

And still, as loud the revel swells,
    The fever'd pulse beats higher,
Till the sear'd taste from foulest wells
    Is fain to slake its fire.

Unlike the feast of heavenly love
    Spread at the Saviour's word

For souls that hear his call, and prove
    Meet for his bridal board.

Why should we fear, youth's draught of joy,
    If pure, would sparkle less?
Why should the cup the sooner cloy,
    Which God hath deign'd to bless?

For, is it Hope, that thrills so keen
    Along each bounding vein,
Still whispering glorious things unseen?—
    Faith makes the vision plain.

The world would kill her soon : but Faith
    Her daring dreams will cherish,
Speeding her gaze o'er time and death
    To realms where nought can perish.

Or is it Love, the dear delight
    Of hearts that know no guile,
That all around see all things bright
    With their own magic smile?

The silent joy, that sinks so deep,
    Of confidence and rest,
Lull'd in a Father's arms to sleep,
    Clasp'd to a Mother's breast?

Who, but a Christian, through all life
    That blessing may prolong?
Who, through the world's sad day of strife,
    Still chant his morning song?

Fathers may hate us or forsake,
    God's foundlings then are we :

Mother on child no pity take ^u,
 But we shall still have Thee.

We may look home, and seek in vain
 A fond fraternal heart,
But Christ hath given his promise plain
 To do a brother's part

Nor shall dull age, as worldlings say,
 The heavenward flame annoy :
The Saviour cannot pass away,
 And with him lives our joy.

Ever the richest tenderest glow
 Sets round th' autumnal sun—
But there sight fails : no heart may know
 The bliss when life is done.

Such is thy banquet, dearest Lord ;
 O give us grace, to cast
Our lot with thine, to trust thy word,
 And keep our best till last.

u Can a woman forget her sucking child, that she should not
have compassion on the son of her womb? yea, they may forget, yet
will I not forget thee. *Isaiah* xlix 15.

Third Sunday after Epiphany.

When Jesus heard it, he marvelled, and said to them that followed, Verily I say unto you, I have not found so great faith, no, not in Israel. St. Matthew viii. 10.

I MARK'D a rainbow in the north,
    What time the wild autumnal sun
From his dark veil at noon look'd forth,
    As glorying in his course half done,
Flinging soft radiance far and wide
Over the dusky heaven and bleak hill-side.

It was a gleam to Memory dear,
    And as I walk and muse apart,
When all seems faithless round and drear,
    I would revive it in my heart,
And watch how light can find its way
To regions farthest from the fount of day.

Light flashes in the gloomiest sky,
    And Music in the dullest plain,
For there the lark is soaring high
    Over her flat and leafless reign,
And chanting in so blithe a tone,
It shames the weary heart to feel itself alone.

Brighter than rainbow in the north,
    More cheery than the matin lark,
Is the soft gleam of Christian worth,
    Which on some holy house we mark ;
Dear to the pastor's aching heart
To think, where'er he looks, such gleam may have a part ;

May dwell, unseen by all but Heaven,
　Like diamond blazing in the mine ;
For ever, where such grace is given,
　It fears in open day to shine [v].
Lest the deep stain it owns within
Break out, and Faith be sham'd by the believer's sin.

In silence and afar they wait,
　To find a prayer their Lord may hear :
Voice of the poor and desolate,
　You best may bring it to his ear.
Your grateful intercessions rise
With more than royal pomp, and pierce the skies.

Happy the soul, whose precious cause
　You in the sovereign Presence plead—
" This is the lover of thy laws [x],
　　" The friend of thine in fear and need "—
For to the poor thy mercy lends
That solemn style, " thy nation and thy friends."

He too is blest, whose outward eye
　The graceful lines of art may trace,
While his free spirit, soaring high,
　Discerns the glorious from the base ;

[v] Lord, .trouble not thyself: for I am not worthy that thou shouldest enter under my roof. *St. Luke* vii. 6.

" From the first time that the impressions of religion settled deeply in his mind, he used great caution to conceal it ; not only in obedience to the rule given by our Saviour, of fasting, praying, and giving alms in secret, but from a particular distrust he had of himself ; for he said he was afraid he should at some time or other do some enormous thing, which if he were looked on as a very religious man, might cast a reproach on the profession of it, and give great advantages to impious men to blaspheme the name of God." *Burnet's Life of Hale, in Wordsworth's Eccl. Biog.* vi. **73.**

[x] He loveth our nation. *St. Luke* vii. 5.

Till out of dust his magic raise [y]
A home for prayer and love, and full harmonious praise,

Where far away and high above,
   In maze on maze the tranced sight
Strays, mindful of that heavenly love
   Which knows no end in depth or height,
While the strong breath of Music seems
To waft us ever on, soaring in blissful dreams.

What though in poor and humble guise
   Thou here didst sojourn, cottage-born?
Yet from thy glory in the skies
   Our earthly gold Thou dost not scorn.
For Love delights to bring her best,
And where Love is, that offering evermore is blest.

Love on the Saviour's dying head
   Her spikenard drops unblam'd may pour,
May mount his cross, and wrap him dead
   In spices from the golden shore [z];
Risen, may embalm his sacred name
With all a Painter's art, and all a Minstrel's flame.

Worthless and lost our offerings seem,
   Drops in the ocean of his praise;
But Mercy with her genial beam
   Is ripening them to pearly blaze,
To sparkle in His crown above,
Who welcomes here a child's as there an angel's love.

[y] He hath built us a synagogue. *St. Luke* vii. 5.
[z] St. John xii 7; xix. 30.

Fourth Sunday after Epiphany. *When they saw him, they besought him that he would depart out of their coasts.* St. Matthew viii. 34.

THEY know th' Almighty's power,
  Who, waken'd by the rushing midnight
    shower,
  Watch for the fitful breeze
To howl and chafe amid the bending trees,
  Watch for the still white gleam
To bathe the landscape in a fiery stream,
  Touching the tremulous eye with sense of light
Too rapid and too pure for all but angel sight.

  They know th' Almighty's love,
Who, when the whirlwinds rock the topmost grove,
  Stand in the shade, and hear
The tumult with a deep exulting fear,
  How, in their fiercest sway,
Curb'd by some power unseen, they die away,
  Like a bold steed that owns his rider's arm,
Proud to be check'd and sooth'd by that o'er-mastering
    charm.

  But there are storms within
That heave the struggling heart with wilder din,
  And there is power and love
The maniac's rushing frenzy to reprove,
  And when he takes his seat,
Cloth'd and in calmness, at his Saviour's feet [a],
  Is not the power as strange, the love as blest,
As when He said, Be still, and ocean sank to rest?

[a] St. Mark v. 15; iv. 39.

Woe to the wayward heart,
That gladlier turns to eye the shuddering start
Of Passion in her might,
Than marks the silent growth of grace and light ;—
Pleas'd in the cheerless tomb
To linger while the morning rays illume
Green lake, and cedar tuft, and spicy glade,
Shaking their dewy tresses now the storm is laid.

The storm is laid—and now
In his meek power He climbs the mountain's brow,
Who bade the waves go sleep,
And lash'd the vex'd fiends to their yawning deep.
How on a rock they stand,
Who watch his eye, and hold his guiding hand !
Not half so fix'd, amid her vassal hills,
Rises the holy pile that Kedron's valley fills.

And wilt thou seek again
Thy howling waste, thy charnel-house and chain,
And with the demons be,
Rather than clasp thine own Deliverer's knee ?
Sure 'tis no heav'n-bred awe
That bids thee from his healing touch withdraw,
The world and He are struggling in thine heart,
And in thy reckless mood thou bidd'st thy Lord depart.

He, merciful and mild,
As erst, beholding, loves his wayward child ;
When souls of highest birth
Waste their impassion'd might on dreams of earth,
He opens Nature's book,
And on his glorious Gospel bids them look,
Till by such chords, as rule the choirs above,
Their lawless cries are tun'd to hymns of perfect love.

Fifth Sunday after Epiphany.

Behold, the Lord's hand is not shortened, that it cannot save; neither his ear heavy, that it cannot hear: But your iniquities have separated between you and your God. Isaiah lix. 1, 2.

" WAKE, arm divine ! awake,
    " Eye of the only Wise !
" Now for thy glory's sake,
    " Saviour and God, arise,
" And may thine ear, that sealed seems,
" In pity mark our mournful themes !"

Thus in her lonely hour
    Thy Church is fain to cry,
As if thy love and power
    Were vanish'd from her sky ;
Yet God is there, and at his side
He triumphs, who for sinners died.

Ah ! 'tis the world enthralls
    The heaven-betrothed breast :
The traitor Sense recalls
    The soaring soul from rest.
That bitter sigh was all for earth,
For glories gone, and vanish'd mirth.

Age would to youth return,
    Farther from heaven would be,
To feel the wildfire burn,
    On idolizing knee
Again to fall, and rob thy shrine
Of hearts, the right of love divine.

Lord of this erring flock !
    Thou whose soft showers distil
On ocean waste or rock,
    Free as on Hermon hill,
Do Thou our craven spirits cheer,
And shame away the selfish tear.

'Twas silent all and dead b
    Beside the barren sea,
Where Philip's steps were led,
    Led by a voice from Thee—
He rose and went, nor ask'd Thee why,
Nor stayed to heave one faithless sigh ;

Upon his lonely way
    The high-born traveller came,
Reading a mournful lay
    Of "One who bore our shame c,
"Silent himself, his name untold,
"And yet his glories were of old."

To muse what Heaven might mean
    His wondering brow he rais'd,
And met an eye serene
    That on him watchful gaz'd.
No Hermit e'er so welcome cross'd
A child's lone path in woodland lost.

Now wonder turns to love ;
    The scrolls of sacred lore
No darksome mazes prove ;
    The desert tires no more :
They bathe where holy waters flow,
Then on their way rejoicing go.

b See Acts viii. 26—40.   c Isaiah liii. 6—8.

They part to meet in heaven ;
 But of the joy they share,
Absolving and forgiven,
 The sweet remembrance bear.
Yes—mark him well, ye cold and proud,
Bewilder'd in a heartless crowd,

 Starting and turning pale
  At Rumour's angry din—
 No storm can now assail
  The charm he wears within,
Rejoicing still, and doing good,
And with the thought of God imbu'd.

 No glare of high estate,
  No gloom of woe or want,
 The radiance can abate
  Where Heaven delights to haunt.
Sin only hides the genial ray,
And, round the Cross, makes night of day.

 Then weep it from thy heart ;
  So may'st thou duly learn
 The intercessor's part,
  Thy prayers and tears may earn
For fallen souls some healing breath,
Ere they have died th' Apostate's death.

Sixth Sunday after Epiphany.

Beloved, now are we the sons of God, and it doth not yet appear what we shall be : but we know that, when he shall appear, we shall be like him ; for we shall see him as he is. 1 John iii. 2.

THERE are, who darkling and alone,
  Would wish the weary night were gone,
Though dawning morn should only shew
The secret of their unknown woe :
Who pray for sharpest throbs of pain
To ease them of doubt's galling chain :
  " Only disperse the cloud," they cry,
" And if our fate be death, give light and let us die d."

  Unwise I deem them, Lord, unmeet
  To profit by thy chastenings sweet,
For thou wouldst have us linger still
Upon the verge of good or ill,
That on thy guiding hand unseen
Our undivided hearts may lean,
  And this our frail and foundering bark
Glide in the narrow wake of thy beloved ark.

  'Tis so in war—the champion true
  Loves victory more, when dim in view
He sees her glories gild afar
The dusky edge of stubborn war,
Than if th' untrodden bloodless field
The harvest of her laurels yield ;
  Let not my bark in calm abide,
But win her fearless way against the chafing tide.

d 'Εν δὲ φάει καὶ ὀλέσσον.

'Tis so in love—the faithful heart
From her dim vision would not part,
When first to her fond gaze is given
That purest spot in Fancy's heaven,
For all the gorgeous sky beside,
Though pledg'd her own and sure t' abide :
Dearer than every past noon-day
That twilight gleam to her, though faint and far away.

So have I seen some tender flower
Priz'd above all the vernal bower,
Shelter'd beneath the coolest shade,
Embosom'd in the greenest glade,
So frail a gem, it scarce may bear
The playful touch of evening air ;
When hardier grown we love it less,
And trust it from our sight, not needing our caress.

And wherefore is the sweet spring tide
Worth all the changeful year beside ?
The last-born babe, why lies its part
Deep in the mother's inmost heart ?
But that the Lord and source of love
Would have his weakest ever prove
Our tenderest care—and most of all
Our frail immortal souls, His work and Satan's thrall.

So be it, Lord ; I know it best,
Though not as yet this wayward breast
Beat quite in answer to thy voice,
Yet surely I have made my choice ;
I know not yet the promis'd bliss,
Know not if I shall win or miss ;
So doubting, rather let me die,
Than close with aught beside, to last eternally.

What is the heaven we idly dream?
The self-deceiver's dreary theme,
A cloudless sun that softly shines,
Bright maidens and unfailing vines,
The warrior's pride, the hunter's mirth,
Poor fragments all of this low earth :
Such as in sleep would hardly soothe
A soul that once had tasted of immortal Truth.

What is the Heaven our God bestows?
No Prophet yet, no Angel knows ;
Was never yet created eye
Could see across Eternity ;
Not seraph's wing for ever soaring
Can pass the flight of souls adoring,
That nearer still and nearer grow
To th' unapproached Lord, once made for them so low.

Unseen, unfelt their earthly growth,
And self-accus'd of sin and sloth
They live and die : their names decay,
Their fragrance passes quite away ;
Like violets in the freezing blast
No vernal steam around they cast,—
But they shall flourish from the tomb,
The breath of God shall wake them into od'rous bloom.

Then on th' incarnate Saviour's breast,
The fount of sweetness, they shall rest,
Their spirits every hour imbu'd
More deeply with his precious blood.
But peace—still voice and closed eye
Suit best with hearts beyond the sky,
Hearts training in their low abode,
Daily to lose themselves in hope to find their God.

Septuagesima Sunday.

The invisible things of him from the creation of the world are clearly seen, being understood by the things that are made. Romans i. 20.

THERE is a book, who runs may read,
  Which heavenly truth imparts,
And all the lore its scholars need,
  Pure eyes and Christian hearts.

The works of God above, below,
  Within us and around,
Are pages in that book, to show
  How God himself is found.

The glorious sky embracing all
  Is like the Maker's love,
Wherewith encompass'd, great and small
  In peace and order move.

The Moon above, the Church below,
  A wondrous race they run,
But all their radiance, all their glow,
  Each borrows of its Sun.

The Saviour lends the light and heat
  That crowns his holy hill ;
The saints, like stars, around his seat,
  Perform their courses still [e].

The saints above are stars in Heaven—
  What are the saints on earth ?

[e] Daniel xii. 3.

Like trees they stand whom God has given [f],
    Our Eden's happy birth.

Faith is their fix'd unswerving root,
    Hope their unfading flower,
Fair deeds of charity their fruit,
    The glory of their bower.

The dew of heaven is like thy grace [g],
    It steals in silence down ;
But where it lights, the favour'd place
    By richest fruits is known.

One Name above all glorious names
    With its ten thousand tongues
The everlasting sea proclaims,
    Echoing angelic songs.

The raging Fire [h], the roaring Wind,
    Thy boundless power display :
But in the gentler breeze we find
    Thy Spirit's viewless way [i].

Two worlds are ours : 'tis only Sin
    Forbids us to descry
The mystic heaven and earth within,
    Plain as the sea and sky.

Thou, who hast given me eyes to see
    And love this sight so fair,
Give me a heart to find out Thee,
    And read Thee every where.

[f] Isaiah lx. 21.   [g] Psalm lxviii. 9.   [h] Hebrews xii. 29.
[i] St. John iii. 8.

Sexagesima Sunday.

So he drove out the man; and he placed at the east of the garden of Eden cherubims, and a flaming sword which turned every way, to keep the way of the tree of life. Genesis iii. 24; compare c. vi.

F OE of mankind ! too bold thy race :
　　Thou runn'st at such a 'reckless pace,
Thine own dire work thou surely wilt confound :
　　'Twas but one little drop of sin
　　We saw this morning enter in,
And lo ! at eventide the world is drown'd.

　　See here the fruit of wandering eyes,
　　Of worldly longings to be wise,
Of Passion dwelling on forbidden sweets :
　　Ye lawless glances, freely rove ;
　　Ruin below and wrath above
Are all that now the wildering fancy meets.

　　Lord, when in some deep garden glade,
　　Of Thee and of myself afraid,
From thoughts like these among the bowers I hide,
　　Nearest and loudest then of all
　　I seem to hear the Judge's call :—
"Where art thou, fallen man ? come forth, and be thou
　　　tried."

　　Trembling before Thee as I stand,
　　Where'er I gaze on either hand
The sentence is gone forth, the ground is curs'd :

Yet mingled with the penal shower
Some drops of balm in every bower
Steal down like April dews, that softest fall and first.

If filial and maternal love [k]
Memorial of our guilt must prove,
If sinful babès in sorrow must be born,
Yet, to assuage her sharpest throes,
The faithful mother surely knows,
This was the way Thou cam'st to save the world forlorn.

If blessed wedlock may not bless [l]
Without some tinge of bitterness
To dash her cup of joy, since Eden lost,
Chaining to earth with strong desire
Hearts that would highest else aspire,
And o'er the tenderer sex usurping ever most ;

Yet by the light of Christian lore
'Tis blind Idolatry no more,
But a sweet help and pattern of true love,
Shewing how best the soul may cling
To her immortal Spouse and King,
How He should rule, and she with full desire approve.

If niggard Earth her treasures hide [m],
To all but labouring hands denied,
Lavish of thorns and worthless weeds alone,
The doom is half in mercy given
To train us in our way to Heaven,
And shew our lagging souls how glory must be won.

[k] In sorrow thou shalt bring forth children. *Gen.* iii. 16.
[l] Thy desire shall be to thy husband, and he shall rule over thee.
Gen. iii. 16.
[m] Cursed is the ground for thy sake. *Gen.* iii. 17.

If on the sinner's outward frame [n]
God hath impress'd his mark of blame,
And even our bodies shrink at touch of light,
  Yet mercy hath not left us bare :
  The very weeds we daily wear [o]
Are to Faith's eye a pledge of God's forgiving might.

And oh ! if yet one arrow more [p],
  The sharpest of th' Almighty's store,
Tremble upon the string—a sinner's death—
  Art Thou not by to soothe and save,
  To lay us gently in the grave,
To close the weary eye and hush the parting breath ?

Therefore in sight of man bereft
  The happy garden still was left,
The fiery sword that guarded shew'd it too,
  Turning all ways, the world to teach,
  That though as yet beyond our reach,
Still in its place the tree of life and glory grew.

[n] I was afraid, because I was naked. *Gen.* iii. 10.

[o] Unto Adam also and to his wife did the Lord God make coats of skins, and clothed them. *Gen.* iii. 21.

[p] Thou shalt surely die. *Gen.* ii. 17.

Quinquagesima Sunday.

I do set my bow in the cloud, and it shall be for a token of a covenant between me and the earth. Genesis ix. 13.

SWEET Dove! the softest, steadiest plume
　　In all the sunbright sky,
Brightening in ever-changeful bloom
　　As breezes change on high ;—

Sweet Leaf! the pledge of peace and mirth,
　　"Long sought, and lately won,"
Bless'd increase of reviving Earth,
　　When first it felt the Sun ;—

Sweet Rainbow! pride of summer days,
　　High set at Heaven's command,
Though into drear and dusky haze
　　Thou melt on either hand ;—

Dear tokens of a pardoning God,
　　We hail ye, one and all,
As when our fathers walk'd abroad,
　　Freed from their twelvemonths' thrall.

How joyful from th' imprisoning ark
　　On the green earth they spring!
Not blither, after showers, the Lark
　　Mounts up with glistening wing.

So home-bound sailors spring to shore,
　　Two oceans safely past ;
So happy souls, when life is o'er,
　　Plunge in th' empyreal vast.

What wins their first and fondest gaze
 In all the blissful field,
And keeps it through a thousand days?
 Love face to face reveal'd :

Love imag'd in that cordial look
 Our Lord in Eden bends
On souls that sin and earth forsook
 In time to die His friends.

And what most welcome and serene
 Dawns on the Patriarch's eye,
In all th' emerging hills so green,
 In all the brightening sky?

What but the gentle rainbow's gleam,
 Soothing the wearied sight,
That cannot bear the solar beam,
 With soft undazzling light?

Lord, if our fathers turn'd to thee
 With such adoring gaze,
Wondering frail man thy light should see
 Without thy scorching blaze.

Where is our love, and where our hearts,
 We who have seen thy Son,
Have tried thy Spirit's winning arts,
 And yet we are not won?

The Son of God in radiance beam'd
 Too bright for us to scan,
But we may face the rays that stream'd
 From the mild Son of Man.

There, parted into rainbow hues,
 In sweet harmonious strife,

We see celestial love diffuse
　　Its light o'er Jesus' life.

God, by His bow, vouchsafes to write
　　This truth in Heaven above ;
As every lovely hue is Light,
　　So every grace is Love.

Ash-Wednesday.

When thou fastest, anoint thine head, and wash thy face ; That thou appear not unto men to fast, but unto thy Father which is in secret.

St. Matthew vi. 17, 18.

"YES—deep within and deeper yet
　　" The rankling shaft of conscience hide,
" Quick let the swelling eye forget
　　" The tears that in the heart abide.
" Calm be the voice, the aspect bold,
　　" No shuddering pass o'er lip or brow,
" For why should Innocence be told
　　" The pangs that guilty spirits bow ?

" The loving eye that watches thine
　　" Close as the air that wraps thee round—
" Why in thy sorrow should it pine,
　　" Since never of thy sin it found ?
" And wherefore should the heathen see q
　　" What chains of darkness thee enslave,
" And mocking say, Lo, this is he
　　" Who own'd a God that could not save ?"

Thus oft the mourner's wayward heart
　　Tempts him to hide his grief and die,
Too feeble for Confession's smart,
　　Too proud to bear a pitying eye ;
How sweet, in that dark hour, to fall
　　On bosoms waiting to receive
Our sighs, and gently whisper all !
　　They love us—will not God forgive ?

q Wherefore should they say among the people, Where is their God ? *Joel* ii. 17.

Else let us keep our fast within,
 Till Heaven and we are quite alone,
Then let the grief,. the shame, the sin,
 Before the mercy-seat be thrown.
Between the porch and altar weep,
 Unworthy of the holiest place,
Yet hoping near the shrine to keep
 One lowly cell in sight of grace.

Nor fear lest sympathy should fail—
 Hast thou not seen, in night-hours drear,
When racking thoughts the heart assail,
 The glimmering stars by turns appear,
And from th' eternal home above
 With silent news of mercy steal?
So Angels pause on tasks of love,
 To look where sorrowing sinners kneel.

Or if no Angel pass that way,
 He who in secret sees, perchance
May bid his own heart-warming ray
 Toward thee stream with kindlier glance,
As when upon His drooping head
 His Father's light was pour'd from Heaven,
What time, unshelter'd and unfed ^r,
 Far in the wild His steps were driven.

High thoughts were with Him in that hour,
 Untold, unspeakable on earth—
And who can stay the soaring power
 Of spirits wean'd from worldly mirth,
While far beyond the sound of praise
 With upward eye they float serene,
And learn to bear their Saviour's blaze
 When Judgment shall undraw the screen?

^r St. Matthew iv. 1.

First Sunday in Lent.

" ANGEL of wrath ! why linger in mid air,
　　" While the devoted city's cry
" Louder and louder swells ? and canst thou spare,
　　" Thy full-charg'd vial standing by ?"
Thus, with stern voice, unsparing Justice pleads :
　　He hears her not—with soften'd gaze
His eye is following where sweet Mercy leads,
And till she give the sign, his fury stays.

Guided by her, along the mountain road,
　　Far through the twilight of the morn,
With hurrying footsteps from th' accurs'd abode
　　He sees the holy household borne :
Angels, or more. on either hand are nigh,
　　To speed them o'er the tempting plain,
Lingering in heart, and with frail sidelong eye
Seeking how near they may unharm'd remain.

" Ah wherefore gleam those upland slopes so fair ?
　　" And why, through every woodland arch,
" Swells yon bright vale, as Eden rich and rare,
　　" Where Jordan winds his stately march ;
" If all must be forsaken, ruin'd all,
　　" If God have planted but to burn ?—
" Surely not yet th' avenging shower will fall,
" Though to my home for one last look I turn."

Thus while they waver, surely long ago
　　They had provoked the withering blast,

But that the merciful Avengers know
　　Their frailty well, and hold them fast.
" Haste, for thy life escape, nor look behind "—
　　Ever in thrilling sounds like these
They check the wandering eye, severely kind,
Nor let the sinner lose his soul at ease.

And when, o'erwearied with the steep ascent,
　　We for a nearer refuge crave,
One little spot of ground in mercy lent,
　　One hour of home before the grave,
Oft in his pity o'er his children weak,
　　His hand withdraws the penal fire,
And where we fondly cling, forbears to wreak
Full vengeance, till our hearts are wean'd entire.

Thus, by the merits of one righteous man,
　　The Church, our Zoar, shall abide,
Till she abuse, so sore, her lengthen'd span,
　　Even Mercy's self her face must hide.
Then, onward yet a step, thou hard-won soul ;
　　Though in the Church thou know thy place,
The mountain farther lies—there seek thy goal,
There breathe at large, o'erpast thy dangerous race.

Sweet is the smile of home ; the mutual look
　　When hearts are of each other sure ;
Sweet all the joys that crowd the household nook,
　　The haunt of all affections pure ;
Yet in the world even these abide, and we
　　Above the world our calling boast :
Once gain the mountain top, and thou art free :
Till then, who rest, presume ; who turn to look, are lost.

Second Sunday in Lent.

And when Esau heard the words of his father, he cried with a great and exceeding bitter cry, and said unto his father, Bless me, even me also, O my father. Genesis xxvii. 34. (Compare Hebrews xii 17. *He found no place of repentance, though he sought it carefully with tears* [s].)

" AND is there in God's world so drear a place
    "Where the loud bitter cry is rais'd in vain?
" Where tears of penance come too late for grace,
    "As on th' uprooted flower the genial rain?"

'Tis even so : the sovereign Lord of souls
    Stores in the dungeon of his boundless realm
Each bolt, that o'er the sinner vainly rolls,
    With gather'd wrath the reprobate to whelm.

Will the storm hear the sailor's piteous cry [t],
    Taught to mistrust, too late, the tempting wave,
When all around he sees but sea and sky,
    A God in anger, a self-chosen grave?

Or will the thorns, that strew intemperance' bed,
    Turn with a wish to down? will late remorse

[s] The author earnestly hopes, that nothing in these stanzas will be understood to express any opinion as to the general efficacy of what is called "a death-bed repentance." Such questions are best left in the merciful obscurity with which Scripture has enveloped them. Esau's probation, as far as his birthright was concerned, was quite over when he uttered the cry in the text. His despondency therefore is not parallel to any thing on this side the grave.

[t] Compare Bp. Butler's Analogy, p. 54—64, ed. 1736.

Recall the shaft the murderer's hand has sped,
    Or from the guiltless bosom turn its course?

Then may th' unbodied soul in safety fleet
    Through the dark curtains of the world above,
Fresh from the stain of crime ; nor fear to meet
    The God, whom here she would not learn to love :

Then is there hope for such as die unblest,
    That angel wings may waft them to the shore,
Nor need th' unready virgin strike her breast,
    Nor wait desponding round the bridegroom's door.

But where is then the stay of contrite hearts?
    Of old they lean'd on thy eternal word,
But with the sinner's fear their hope departs,
    Fast link'd as thy great Name to Thee, O Lord :

That Name, by which thy faithful oath is past,
    That we should endless be, for joy or woe :—
And if the treasures of thy wrath could waste,
    Thy lovers must their promis'd Heaven forego.

But ask of elder days, earth's vernal hour,
    When in familiar talk God's voice was heard,
When at the Patriarch's call the fiery shower
    Propitious o'er the turf-built shrine appear'd.

Watch by our father Isaac's pastoral door—
    The birthright sold, the blessing lost and won,
Tell, Heaven has wrath that can relent no more,
    The Grave, dark deeds that cannot be undone.

We barter life for pottage ; sell true bliss
    For wealth or power, for pleasure or renown ;
Thus, Esau-like, our Father's blessing miss,
    Then wash with fruitless tears our faded crown.

Our faded crown, despis'd and flung aside,
 Shall on some brother's brow immortal bloom,
No.partial hand the blessing may misguide ;
 No flattering fancy change our Monarch's doom :

His righteous doom, that meek true-hearted Love
 The everlasting birthright should receive,
The softest dews drop on her from above [u],
 The richest green her mountain garland weave :

Her brethren, mightiest, wisest, eldest-born,
 Bow to her sway, and move at her behest :
Isaac's fond blessing may not fall on scorn,
 Nor Balaam's curse on Love, which God hath blest.

[u] Genesis xxvii. 27, 28.

When a strong man armed keepeth his palace, his goods are in peace: But when a stronger than he shall come upon him, and overcome him, he taketh from him all his armour wherein he trusted, and divideth his spoils. St. Luke xi. 21, 22.

SEE Lucifer like lightning fall
    Dash'd from his throne of pride ;
While, answering Thy victorious call,
    The Saints his spoils divide,
This world of thine, by him usurp'd too long,
Now opening all her stores to heal thy servants' wrong.

So when the first-born of thy foes
    Dead in the darkness lay,
When thy redeem'd at midnight rose
    And cast their bonds away,
The orphan'd realm threw wide her gates, and told
Into freed Israel's lap her jewels and her gold.

And when their wondrous march was o'er,
    And they had won their homes,
Where Abraham fed his flock of yore,
    Among their fathers' tombs ;—
A land that drinks the rain of heaven at will,
Whose waters kiss the feet of many a vine-clad hill ;—

Oft as they watch'd, at thoughtful eve,
    A gale from bowers of balm
Sweep o'er the billowy corn, and heave
    The tresses of the palm,
Just as the lingering Sun had touch'd with gold,
Far o'er the cedar shade, some tower of giants old ;

It was a fearful joy, I ween,
    To trace the Heathen's toil,
The limpid wells, the orchards green
    Left ready for the spoil,
The household stores untouch'd, the roses bright
Wreath'd o'er the cottage walls in garlands of delight.

And now another Canaan yields
    To thine all-conquering ark ;—
Fly from the " old poetic " fields [x],
    Ye Paynim shadows dark !
Immortal Greece, dear land of glorious lays,
Lo ! here the " unknown God" of thy unconscious praise!

The olive wreath, the ivied wand,
    " The sword in myrtles drest,"
Each legend of the shadowy strand
    Now wakes a vision blest :
As little children lisp, and tell of Heaven,
So thoughts beyond their thought to those high Bards
      were given.

And these are ours : Thy partial grace
    The tempting treasure lends :
These relics of a guilty race
    Are forfeit to thy friends :
What seem'd an idol hymn, now breathes of Thee,
Tun'd by Faith's ear to some celestial melody.

There's not a strain to Memory dear [y],
    Nor flower in classic grove,
There's not a sweet note warbled here,
    But minds us of thy Love.
O Lord, our Lord, and spoiler of our foes,
There is no light but thine : with Thee all beauty glows.

[x] Where each old poetic mountain
    Inspiration breathed around. *Gray.*
[y] See Burns's Works, i. 293. Dr. Currie's edition.

Fourth Sunday in Lent.

WHEN Nature tries her finest touch,
        Weaving her vernal wreath,
Mark ye, how close she veils her round,
Not to be trac'd by sight or sound,
        Nor soil'd by ruder breath?

Who ever saw the earliest rose
        First open her sweet breast?
Or, when the summer sun goes down,
The first soft star in evening's crown
        Light up her gleaming crest?

Fondly we seek the dawning bloom
        On features wan and fair,—
The gazing eye no change can trace,
But look away a little space,
        Then turn, and, lo ! 'tis there.

But there's a sweeter flower than e'er
        Blush'd on the rosy spray—
A brighter star, a richer bloom
Than e'er did western heaven illume
        At close of summer day.

'Tis Love, the last best gift of Heaven ;
　　Love gentle, holy, pure :
But tenderer than a dove's soft eye,
The searching sun, the open sky,
　　She never could endure.

Even human Love will shrink from sight
　　Here in the coarse rude earth :
How then should rash intruding glance
Break in upon *her* sacred trance
　　Who boasts a heavenly birth ?

So still and secret is her growth,
　　Ever the truest heart,
Where deepest strikes her kindly root
For hope or joy, for flower or fruit,
　　Least knows its happy part.

God only, and good angels, look
　　Behind the blissful screen—
As when, triumphant o'er his woes,
The Son of God by moonlight rose,
　　By all but Heaven unseen :

As when the holy Maid beheld
　　Her risen Son and Lord :
Thought has not colours half so fair
That she to paint that hour may dare,
　　In silence best ador'd.

The gracious Dove, that brought from Heaven
　　The earnest of our bliss,
Of many a chosen witness telling,
On many a happy vision dwelling,
　　Sings not a note of this.

So, truest image of the Christ,
    Old Israel's long-lost son,
What time, with sweet forgiving cheer,
He call'd his conscious brethren near,
    Would weep with them alone.

He could not trust his melting soul
    But in his Maker's sight—
Then why should gentle hearts and true
Bare to the rude world's withering view
    Their treasure of delight !

No—let the dainty rose awhile
    Her bashful fragrance hide—
Rend not her silken veil too soon,
But leave her, in her own soft noon,
    To flourish and abide.

Fifth Sunday in Lent.

And Moses said, I will now turn aside, and see this great sight, why the bush is not burnt. Exodus iii. 3.

TH' historic Muse, from age to age,
Thro' many a waste heart-sickening page
    Hath trac'd the works of Man :
But a celestial call to-day
Stays her, like Moses, on her way,
    The works of God to scan.

Far seen across the sandy wild,
Where, like a solitary child,
    He thoughtless roam'd and free,
One towering thorn [z] was wrapt in flame—
Bright without blaze it went and came :
    Who would not turn and see ?

Along the mountain ledges green
The scatter'd sheep at will may glean
    The Desert's spicy stores :
The while, with undivided heart,
The shepherd talks with God apart,
    And, as he talks, adores.

Ye too, who tend Christ's wildering flock,
Well may ye gather round the rock
    That once was Sion's hill :
To watch the fire upon the mount
Still blazing, like the solar fount,
    Yet unconsuming still.

[z] " Seneh ;" said to be a sort of Acacia.

Caught from that blaze by wrath divine,
Lost branches of the once-lov'd vine,
    Now wither'd, spent, and sere,
See Israel's sons, like glowing brands,
Tost wildly o'er a thousand lands
    For twice a thousand year.

God will not quench nor slay them quite,
But lifts them like a beacon light
    Th' apostate Church to scare;
Or like pale ghosts that darkling roam,
Hovering around their ancient home,
    But find no refuge there.

Ye blessed Angels! if of you
There be, who love the ways to view
    Of Kings and Kingdoms here;
And sure, 'tis worth an Angel's gaze,
To see, throughout that dreary maze,
    God teaching love and fear:

Oh say, in all the bleak expanse,
Is there a spot to win your glance,
    So bright, so dark as this?
A hopeless faith, a homeless race,
Yet seeking the most holy place,
    And owning the true bliss!

Salted with fire they seem [a], to show
How spirits lost in endless woe
    May undecaying live.
Oh sickening thought! yet hold it fast
Long as this glittering world shall last,
    Or sin at heart survive.

[a] St. Mark ix. 49.

And hark ! amid the flashing fire,
Mingling with tones of fear and ire,
      Soft Mercy's undersong—
'Tis Abraham's God who speaks so loud,
His people's cries have pierc'd the cloud,
      He sees, He sees their wrong [b];

He is come down to break their chain ;
Though never more on Sion's fane
      His visible ensign wave ;
'Tis Sion, wheresoe'er they dwell,
Who, with His own true Israel,
      Shall own Him strong to save.

He shall redeem them one by one,
Where'er the world-encircling sun
      Shall see them meekly kneel :
All that He asks on Israel's part,
Is only, that the captive heart
      Its woe and burthen feel.

Gentiles ! with fix'd yet awful eye
Turn ye this page of mystery,
      Nor slight the warning sound :
" Put off thy shoes from off thy feet—
" The place where man his God shall meet,
      " Be sure, is holy ground."

      [b] Exodus iii. 7, 8.

Palm Sunday.

YE whose hearts are beating high
   With the pulse of Poesy,
Heirs of more than royal race,
Fram'd by Heaven's peculiar grace,
God's own work to do on earth,
   If the word be not too bold,
Giving virtue a new birth,
   And a life that ne'er grows old—

Sovereign masters of all hearts !
Know ye, who hath set your parts ?
He who gave you breath to sing,
By whose strength ye sweep the string,
He hath chosen you, to lead
   His Hosannas here below ;—
Mount, and claim your glorious meed ;
   Linger not with sin and woe.

But if ye should hold your peace,
Deem not that the song would cease—
Angels round His glory-throne,
Stars, His guiding hand that own,
Flowers, that grow beneath our feet,
   Stones in earth's dark womb that rest,
High and low in choir shall meet,
   Ere His Name shall be unblest.

Lord, by every minstrel tongue
Be thy praise so duly sung,

That thine angels' harps may ne'er
Fail to find fit echoing here :
We the while, of meaner birth,
   Who in that divinest spell
Dare not hope to join on earth,
   Give us grace to listen well.

But should thankless silence seal
Lips; that might half Heaven reveal,
Should bards in idol-hymns profane
The sacred soul-enthralling strain,—
As in this bad world below
   Noblest things find vilest using,—
Then, thy power and mercy show,
   In vile things noble breath infusing ;

Then waken into sound divine
The very pavement of thy shrine,
Till we, like Heaven's star-sprinkled floor,
Faintly give back what we adore.
Childlike though the voices be,
   And untunable the parts,
Thou wilt own the minstrelsy,
   If it flow from childlike hearts.

Monday before Easter.

Doubtless thou art our father, though Abraham be ignorant of us, and Israel acknowledge us not. Isaiah lxiii. 16.

" FATHER to me Thou art and Mother dear,
      "And Brother too, kind husband of my heart"—
So speaks Andromache ^c in boding fear,
      Ere from her last embrace her hero part—
So evermore, by Faith's undying glow,
We own the Crucified in weal or woe.

Strange to our ears the church-bells of our home,
      The fragrance of our old paternal fields
May be forgotten ; and the time may come
      When the babe's kiss no sense of pleasure yields
Even to the doting mother : but thine own
Thou never canst forget, nor leave alone.

There are who sigh that no fond heart is theirs,
      None loves them best—O vain and selfish sigh !
Out of the bosom of His love He spares—
      The Father spares the Son, for thee to die :
For thee He died—for thee He lives again :
O'er thee He watches in His boundless reign.

Thou art as much His care, as if beside
      Nor man nor angel liv'd in heaven or earth :
Thus sunbeams pour alike their glorious tide
      To light up worlds, or wake an insect's mirth :
They shine and shine with unexhausted store—
Thou art thy Saviour's darling—seek no more.

^c Iliad, vi. 429.

On thee and thine, thy warfare and thine end,
  Even in His hour of agony He thought,
When, ere the final pang His soul should rend,
  The ransom'd spirits one by one were brought
To his mind's eye—two silent nights and days d
In calmness for His far-seen hour He stays.

Ye vaulted cells where martyr'd seers of old
  Far in the rocky walls of Sion sleep,
Green terraces and arched fountains cold,
  Where lies the cypress shade so still and deep,
Dear sacred haunts of glory and of woe,
Help us, one hour, to trace His musings high and low :

One heart-ennobling hour ! It may not be :
  Th' unearthly thoughts have pass'd from earth away,
And fast as evening sunbeams from the sea
  Thy footsteps all in Sion's deep decay
Were blotted from the holy ground : yet dear
Is every stone of hers ; for Thou wast surely here.

There is a spot within this sacred dale
  That felt Thee kneeling—touch'd thy prostrate brow :
One angel knows it.   O might prayer avail
  To win that knowledge ! sure each holy vow
Less quickly from th' unstable soul would fade,
Offer'd where Christ in agony was laid.

Might tear of ours once mingle with the blood
  That from His aching brow by moonlight fell,
Over the mournful joy our thoughts would brood,
  Till they had fram'd within a guardian spell

---

d In Passion week, from Tuesday evening to Thursday evening :
during which time Scripture seems to be nearly silent concerning
our Saviour's proceedings.

To chase repining fancies, as they rise,
Like birds of evil wing, to mar our sacrifice.

So dreams the heart self-flattering, fondly dreams ;—
 Else wherefore, when the bitter waves o'erflow,
Miss we the light, Gethsemane, that streams
 From thy dear name, where in His page of woe
It shines, a pale kind star in winter's sky ?
Who vainly reads it there, in vain had seen Him die.

Tuesday before Easter.

They gave him to drink wine mingled with myrrh : but he received it not.
St. Mark xv. 23.

" FILL high the bowl, and spice it well, and pour
" The dews oblivious : for the Cross is sharp,
    " The Cross is sharp, and He
    " Is tenderer than a lamb.

" He wept by Lazarus' grave—how will He bear
" This bed of anguish ? and his pale weak form
    " Is worn with many a watch
    " Of sorrow and unrest.

" His sweat last night was as great drops of blood,
" And the sad burthen press'd him so to earth,
    " The very torturers paus'd
    " To help Him on His way.

" Fill high the bowl, benumb His aching sense
" With medicin'd sleep."—O awful in thy woe !
    The parching thirst of death
    Is on thee, and thou triest

The slumbrous potion bland, and wilt not drink :
Not sullen, nor in scorn, like haughty man
    With suicidal hand
    Putting his solace by :

But as at first thine all-pervading look
Saw from thy Father's bosom to th' abyss,
    Measuring in calm presage
    The infinite descent ;

So to the end, though now of mortal pangs
Made heir, and emptied of thy glory awhile,
    With unaverted eye
    Thou meetest all the storm.

Thou wilt feel all, that Thou may'st pity all ;
And rather wouldst Thou wrestle with strong pain,
    Than overcloud thy soul,
    So clear in agony,

Or lose one glimpse of Heaven before the time.
O most entire and perfect sacrifice,
    Renew'd in every pulse
    That on the tedious Cross

Told the long hours of death, as, one by one,
The life-strings of that tender heart gave way ;
    Even sinners, taught by Thee,
    Look Sorrow in the face,

And bid her freely welcome, unbeguil'd
By false kind solaces, and spells of earth :—
    And yet not all unsooth'd ;
    For when was Joy so dear,

As the deep calm that breath'd, " *Father, forgive,*"
Or, " *Be with me in Paradise to-day !*"
    And, though the strife be sore,
    Yet in His parting breath

Love masters agony ; the soul that seem'd
Forsaken, feels her present God again,
    And in her Father's arms
    Contented dies away.

Wednesday before Easter

Saying, Father, if thou be willing, remove this cup from me: nevertheless not my will, but thine, be done. St. Luke xxii. 42.

O LORD my God, do Thou thy holy will—
    I will lie still—
I will not stir, lest I forsake thine arm,
    And break the charm,
Which lulls me, clinging to my Father's breast,
    In perfect rest.

Wild Fancy, peace! thou must not me beguile
    With thy false smile :
I know thy flatteries and thy cheating ways ;
    Be silent, Praise,
Blind guide with siren voice, and blinding all
    That hear thy call.

Come, Self-devotion, high and pure,
Thoughts that in thankfulness endure,
Though dearest hopes are faithless found,
And dearest hearts are bursting round.
Come, Resignation, spirit meek,
And let me kiss thy placid cheek,
And read in thy pale eye serene
Their blessing, who by faith can wean
Their hearts from sense, and learn to love
God only, and the joys above.

They say, who know the life divine,
And upward gaze with eagle eyne,
That by each golden crown on high [e],
Rich with celestial jewelry,

[e] ". . . that little coronet or special reward which God hath prepared (extraordinary and besides the great Crown of all faithful

Which for our Lord's redeem'd is set,
There hangs a radiant coronet,
All gemm'd with pure and living light,
Too dazzling for a sinner's sight,
Prepar'd for virgin souls, and them
Who seek the martyr's diadem.

Nor deem, who to that bliss aspire,
Must win their way through blood and fire.
The writhings of a wounded heart
Are fiercer than a foeman's dart.
Oft in Life's stillest shade reclining,
In Desolation unrepining,
Without a hope on earth to find
A mirror in an answering mind,
Meek souls there are, who little dream
Their daily strife an Angel's theme,
Or that the rod they take so calm
Shall prove in Heaven a martyr's palm.

And there are souls that seem to dwell
Above this earth—so rich a spell
Floats round their steps, where'er they move,
From hopes fulfill'd and mutual love.
Such, if on high their thoughts are set,
Nor in the stream the source forget,
If prompt to quit the bliss they know,
Following the Lamb where'er he go,
By purest pleasures unbeguil'd
To idolize or wife or child ;
Such wedded souls our God shall own
For faultless virgins round his throne.

souls) for those ' who have not defiled themselves with women, but
follow the (virgin) Lamb for ever.' " *Bp. Taylor, Holy Living,* c.
xi. sect. 3.

Thus every where we find our suffering God,
    And where He trod
May set our steps : the Cross on Calvary
    Uplifted high
Beams on the martyr host, a beacon light
    In open fight.

To the still wrestlings of the lonely heart
    He doth impart
The virtue of His midnight agony,
    When none was nigh,
Save God and one good angel, to assuage
    The tempest's rage.

Mortal ! if life smile on thee, and thou find
    All to thy mind,
Think, who did once from Heaven to Hell descend
    Thee to befriend :
So shalt thou dare forego, at His dear call,
    Thy best, thine all.

" O Father ! not my will, but thine be done "—
    So spake the Son.
Be this our charm, mellowing Earth's ruder noise
    Of griefs and joys ;
That we may cling for ever to thy breast
    In perfect rest !

Thursday before Easter.

At the beginning of thy supplications the commandment came forth, and I am come to shew thee; for thou art greatly beloved: therefore understand the matter, and consider the vision. Daniel ix. 23.

"O HOLY mountain of my God,
    " How do thy towers in ruin lie,
" How art thou riven and strewn abroad,
    " Under the rude and wasteful sky !"
'Twas thus upon his fasting-day
The "Man of Loves" was fain to pray,
His lattice open f toward his darling west,
Mourning the ruin'd home he still must love the best.

Oh for a love like Daniel's now,
    To wing to Heaven but one strong prayer
For God's new Israel, sunk as low,
    Yet flourishing to sight as fair,
As Sion in her height of pride,
With queens for handmaids at her side,
With kings her nursing-fathers, throned high,
And compass'd with the world's too tempting blazonry.

'Tis true, nor winter stays thy growth,
    Nor torrid summer's sickly smile ;
The flashing billows of the south
    Break not upon so lone an isle,
But thou, rich vine, art grafted there,
The fruit of death or life to bear,
Yielding a surer witness every day,
To thine Almighty Author and his stedfast sway.

f Daniel vi. 10.

Oh grief to think, that grapes of gall
    Should cluster round thine healthiest shoot !
God's herald prove a heartless thrall,
    Who, if he dar'd, would fain be mute !
Even such is this bad world we see,
Which, self-condemn'd in owning Thee,
  Yet dares not open farewell of Thee take,
For very pride, and her high-boasted Reason's sake.

What do we then ? if far and wide
    Men kneel to Christ, the pure and meek,
Yet rage with passion, swell with pride,
    Have we not still our faith to seek ?
Nay—but in stedfast humbleness
Kneel on to Him, who loves to bless
The prayer that waits for Him ; and trembling strive
To keep the lingering flame in thine own breast alive.

Dark frown'd the future even on him,
    The loving and beloved Seer,
What time he saw, through shadows dim,
    The boundary of th' eternal year ;
He only of the sons of men
Nam'd to be heir of glory then [g].
Else had it bruis'd too sore his tender heart
To see God's ransom'd world in wrath and flame depart.

Then look no more : or closer watch
    Thy course in Earth's bewildering ways,
For every glimpse thine eye can catch
    Of what shall be in those dread days :
So when th' Archangel's word is spoken,
And Death's deep trance for ever broken,
In mercy thou may'st feel the heavenly hand,
And in thy lot unharm'd before thy Saviour stand [h].

[g] Daniel xii. 13. See Bp. Kenn's Sermon on the character of
Daniel.

[h] Thou shalt rest, and stand in thy lot at the end of the days.
Daniel xii. 13.

Good Friday.

He is despised and rejected of men. Isaiah liii. 3.

IS it not strange, the darkest hour
 That ever dawn'd on sinful earth
Should touch the heart with softer power
 For comfort, than an angel's mirth?
That to the Cross the mourner's eye should turn
Sooner than where the stars of Christmas burn?

Sooner than where the Easter sun
 Shines glorious on yon open grave,
And to and fro the tidings run,
 " Who died to heal, is ris'n to save?"
Sooner than where upon the Saviour's friends
The very Comforter in light and love descends.

Yet so it is : for duly there
 The bitter herbs of earth are set,
Till temper'd by the Saviour's prayer,
 And with the Saviour's life-blood wet,
They turn to sweetness, and drop holy balm,
Soft as imprison'd martyr's death-bed calm.

All turn to sweet—but most of all
 That bitterest to the lip of pride,
When hopes presumptuous fade and fall,
 Or Friendship scorns us, duly tried,
Or Love, the flower that closes up for fear
When rude and selfish spirits breathe too near.

Then like a long-forgotten strain
 Comes sweeping o'er the heart forlorn
What sunshine hours had taught in vain
 Of Jesus suffering shame and scorn.

As in all lowly hearts he suffers still,
While we triumphant ride and have the world at will.

His pierced hands in vain would hide
    His face from rude reproachful gaze,
His ears are open to abide
    The wildest storm the tongue can raise,
He who with one rough word [i], some early day,
Their idol world and them shall sweep for aye away.

But we by Fancy may assuage
    The festering sore by Fancy made,
Down in some lonely hermitage
    Like wounded pilgrims safely laid.
Where gentlest breezes whisper souls distress'd,
That Love yet lives, and Patience shall find rest.

O shame beyond the bitterest thought
    That evil spirit ever fram'd,
That sinners know what Jesus wrought,
    Yet feel their haughty hearts untam'd—
That souls in refuge, holding by the Cross,
Should wince and fret at this world's little loss.

Lord of my heart, by Thy last cry,
    Let not thy blood on earth be spent—
Lo, at thy feet I fainting lie,
    Mine eyes upon thy wounds are bent,
Upon thy streaming wounds my weary eyes
Wait like the parched earth on April skies.

Wash me, and dry these bitter tears,
    O let my heart no further roam,
'Tis thine by vows, and hopes, and fears,
    Long since—O call thy wanderer home ;
To that dear home, safe in Thy wounded side,
Where only broken hearts their sin and shame may
        hide.

[i] Wisdom of Solomon xii. 9.

Easter Eve.

As for thee also, by the blood of thy covenant I have sent forth thy prisoners out of the pit wherein is no water.
Zechariah ix. 11.

AT length the worst is o'er, and Thou art laid
    Deep in thy darksome bed ;
All still and cold beneath yon dreary stone
    Thy sacred form is gone ;
Around those lips where power and mercy hung,
    The dews of death have clung ;
The dull earth o'er Thee, and thy foes around,
Thou sleep'st a silent corse, in funeral fetters wound.

Sleep'st Thou indeed ? or is thy spirit fled,
    At large among the dead ?
Whether in Eden bowers thy welcome voice
    Wake Abraham to rejoice,
Or in some drearier scene thine eye controuls
    The thronging band of souls ;
That, as thy blood won earth, thine agony
Might set the shadowy realm from sin and sorrow free.

Where'er Thou roam'st, one happy soul, we know,
    Seen at thy side in woe [j],
Waits on thy triumph—even as all the blest
    With him and thee shall rest.
Each on his cross, by Thee we hang a while,
    Watching thy patient smile,
Till we have learn'd to say, "'Tis justly done,
" Only in glory, Lord, thy sinful servant own."

[j] St. Luke xxiii. 43.

Soon wilt Thou take us to thy tranquil bower
　　To rest one little hour,
Till thine elect are number'd, and the grave
　　Call Thee to come and save :
Then on thy bosom borne shall we descend,
　　Again with earth to blend,
Earth all refin'd with bright supernal fires,
Tinctur'd with holy blood, and wing'd with pure desires.

Meanwhile with every son and saint of thine
　　Along the glorious line,
Sitting by turns beneath thy sacred feet
　　We'll hold communion sweet,
Know them by look and voice, and thank them all
　　For helping us in thrall,
For words of hope, and bright examples given
To shew through moonless skies that there is light in
　　　　Heaven.

O come that day, when in this restless heart
　　Earth shall resign her part,
When in the grave with Thee my limbs shall rest,
　　My soul with Thee be blest !
But stay, presumptuous—Christ with thee abides
　　In the rock's dreary sides :
He from the stone will wring celestial dew
If but the prisoner's heart be faithful found and true.

When tears are spent, and thou art left alone
　　With ghosts of blessings gone,
Think thou art taken from the cross, and laid
　　In Jesus' burial shade ;
Take Moses' rod, the rod of prayer, and call
　　Out of the rocky wall
The fount of holy blood ; and lift on high
Thy grovelling soul that feels so desolate and dry.

Prisoner of Hope thou art [k]—look up and sing
       In hope of promis'd spring.
As in the pit his father's darling lay [l]
       Beside the desert way,
And knew not how, but knew his God would save
       Even from that living grave,
So, buried with our Lord, we'll close our eyes
To the decaying world, till Angels bid us rise.

[k] Turn you to the strong hold, ye prisoners of hope. *Zechariah* ix. 12.

[l] They took him, and cast him into a pit : and the pit was empty, there was no water in it. *Genesis* xxxvii. 24.

Easter Day.

OH ! day of days ! shall hearts set free
    No " minstrel rapture " find for Thee ?
Thou art the Sun of other days,
They shine by giving back thy rays :

Enthroned in thy sovereign sphere
Thou shedd'st thy light on all the year ;
Sundays by Thee more glorious break,
An Easter Day in every week :

And week-days, following in their train,
The fulness of thy blessing gain,
Till all, both resting and employ,
Be one Lord's day of holy joy.

Then wake, my soul, to high desires,
And earlier light thine altar fires :
The World some hours is on her way,
Nor thinks on thee, thou blessed day :

Or, if she think, it is in scorn :
The vernal light of Easter morn
To her dark gaze no brighter seems
Than Reason's or the Law's pale beams.

" Where is your Lord ?" she scornful asks :
" Where is his hire ? we know his tasks ;
" Sons of a king ye boast to be ;
" Let us your crowns and treasures see. "

We in the words of Truth reply,
An angel brought them from the sky,
" Our crown, our treasure is not here,
" 'Tis stored above the highest sphere :

" Methinks your wisdom guides amiss,
" To seek on earth a Christian's bliss ;
" We watch not now the lifeless stone ;
" Our only Lord is risen and gone."

Yet even the lifeless stone is dear
For thoughts of Him who late lay here ;
And the base world, now Christ hath died,
Ennobled is and glorified.

No more a charnel-house, to fence
The relics of lost innocence,
A vault of ruin and decay ;—
Th' imprisoning stone is roll'd away :

'Tis now a cell, where angels use
To come and go with heavenly news,
And in the ears of mourners say,
" Come, see the place where Jesus lay :"

'Tis now a fane, where Love can find
Christ every where embalm'd and shrin'd ;
Aye gathering up memorials sweet,
Where'er she sets her duteous feet.

Oh ! joy to Mary first allow'd,
When rous'd from weeping o'er his shroud,
By his own calm, soul-soothing tone,
Breathing her name, as still his own !

Joy to the faithful Three renew'd,
As their glad errand they pursued !

Happy, who so Christ's word convey,
That he may meet them on their way !

So is it still : to holy tears,
In lonely hours, Christ risen appears :
In social hours, who Christ would see,
Must turn all tasks to Charity.

Monday in Easter Week.

Of a truth I perceive that God is no respecter of persons: But in every nation he that feareth him, and worketh righteousness, is accepted with him. Acts x. 34, 35.

G O up and watch the new-born rill
  Just trickling from its mossy bed,
    Streaking the heath-clad hill
      With a bright emerald thread.

Canst thou her bold career foretel,
  What rocks she shall o'erleap or rend,
    How far in Ocean's swell,
      Her freshening billows send?

Perchance that little brook shall flow
  The bulwark of some mighty realm,
    Bear navies to and fro
      With monarchs at their helm.

Or canst thou guess, how far away
  Some sister nymph, beside her urn
    Reclining night and day,
      Mid reeds and mountain fern,

Nurses her store, with thine to blend
  When many a moor and glen are past,
    Then in the wide sea end
      Their spotless lives at last?

Even so, the course of prayer who knows?
  It springs in silence where it will,

8

Springs out of sight, and flows
At first a lonely rill :

But streams shall meet it by and by
From thousand sympathetic hearts,
Together swelling high
Their chant of many parts.

Unheard by all but angel ears
The good Cornelius knelt alone,
Nor dream'd his prayers and tears
Would help a world undone.

The while upon his terrac'd roof
The lov'd Apostle to his Lord
In silent thought aloof
For heavenly vision soar'd.

Far o'er the glowing western main
His wistful brow was upward rais'd,
Where, like an angel's train,
The burnish'd water blaz'd.

The saint beside the ocean pray'd,
The soldier in his chosen bower,
Where all his eye survey'd
Seem'd sacred in that hour.

To each unknown his brother's prayer,
Yet brethren true in dearest love
Were they—and now they share
Fraternal joys above.

There daily through Christ's open gate
They see the Gentile spirits press,

Brightening their high estate
With dearer happiness.

What civic wreath for comrades sav'd
Shone ever with such deathless gleam,
Or when did perils brav'd
So sweet to veterans seem?

Tuesday in Easter Week.

And they departed quickly from the sepulchre with fear and great joy; and did run to bring his disciples word. St. Matthew xxviii. 8.

TO THE SNOW-DROP.

THOU first-born of the year's delight,
 Pride of the dewy glade,
In vernal green and virgin white,
 Thy vestal robes, array'd :

'Tis not because thy drooping form
 Sinks graceful on its nest,
When chilly shades from gathering storm
 Affright thy tender breast ;

Nor for yon river islet wild
 Beneath the willow spray,
Where, like the ringlets of a child,
 Thou weav'st thy circle gay ;

'Tis not for these I love thee dear—
 Thy shy averted smiles
To Fancy bode a joyous year,
 One of Life's fairy isles.

They twinkle to the wintry moon,
 And cheer th' ungenial day,
And tell us, all will glisten soon
 As green and bright as they.

Is there a heart, that loves the spring,
 Their witness can refuse ?

Yet mortals doubt, when angels bring
  From Heaven their Easter news :

When holy maids and matrons speak
  Of Christ's forsaken bed,
And voices, that forbid to seek
  The living mid the dead,

And when they say, "Turn wandering heart,
  "Thy Lord is ris'n indeed,
"Let Pleasure go, put Care apart,
  "And to His presence speed ;"

We smile in scorn : and yet we know
  They early sought the tomb,
Their hearts, that now so freshly glow,
  Lost in desponding gloom.

They who have sought. nor hope to find,
  Wear not so bright a glance :
They, who have won their earthly mind,
  Less reverently advance.

But where, in gentle spirits, fear
  And joy so duly meet,
These sure have seen the angels near,
  And kiss'd the Saviour's feet.

Nor let the Pastor's thankful eye
  Their faltering tale disdain,
As on their lowly couch they lie,
  Prisoners of want and pain.

O guide us, when our faithless hearts
  From Thee would start aloof,

Where Patience her sweet skill imparts
   Beneath some cottage roof :

Revive our dying fires, to burn
   High as her anthems soar,
And of our scholars let us learn
   Our own forgotten lore.

First Sunday after Easter.

Seemeth it but a small thing unto you, that the God of Israel hath separated you from the congregation of Israel, to bring you near to himself?

Numbers xvi. 9.

FIRST Father of the holy seed,
If yet, invok'd in hour of need,
Thou 'count me for thine own,
Not quite an outcast if I prove,
Thou joy'st in miracles of love,
Hear, from thy mercy-throne !

Upon thine altar's horn of gold
Help me to lay my trembling hold,
Though stain'd with Christian gore ;—
The blood of souls by Thee redeem'd,
But, while I rov'd or idly dream'd,
Lost to be found no more.

For oft, when summer leaves were bright,
And every flower was bath'd in light,
In sunshine moments past,
My wilful heart would burst away
From where the holy shadow lay,
Where Heaven my lot had cast.

I thought it scorn with Thee to dwell,
A Hermit in a silent cell,
While, gaily sweeping by,
Wild Fancy blew his bugle strain,
And marshall'd all his gallant train
In the world's wondering eye.

I would have join'd him—but as oft
Thy whisper'd warnings, kind and soft,
  My better soul confess'd.
" My servant, let the world alone,
" Safe on the steps of Jesus' throne
  " Be tranquil and be blest.

" Seems it to thee a niggard hand
" That nearest Heaven has bade thee stand,
  " The ark to touch and bear,
" With incense of pure heart's desire
" To heap the censer's sacred fire,
  " The snow-white Ephod wear ?"

Why should we crave the worldling's wreath,
On whom the Saviour deign'd to breathe,
  To whom his keys were given,
Who lead the choir where angels meet,
With angels' food our brethren greet,
  And pour the drink of Heaven?

When sorrow all our heart would ask,
We need not shun our daily task,
  And hide ourselves for calm ;
The herbs we seek to heal our woe
Familiar by our pathway grow,
  Our common air is balm.

Around each pure domestic shrine
Bright flowers of Eden bloom and twine,
  Our hearths are altars all ;
The prayers of hungry souls and poor,
Like armed angels at the door,
  Our unseen foes appal.

Alms all around and hymns within—
What evil eye can entrance win

Where guards like these abound ?
If chance some heedless heart should roam,
Sure, thought of these will lure it home
 Ere lost in Folly's round.

O joys, that sweetest in decay,
Fall not, like wither'd leaves, away,
 But with the silent breath
Of violets drooping one by one,
Soon as their fragrant task is done,
 Are wafted high in death !

Second Sunday after Easter.

He hath said, which heard the words of God, and knew the knowledge of the most High, which saw the vision of the Almighty, falling into a trance, but having his eyes open: I shall see him, but not now: I shall behold him, but not nigh: there shall come a Star out of Jacob, and a Sceptre shall rise out of Israel, and shall smite the corners of Moab, and destroy all the children of Sheth. Numbers xxiv. 16, 17.

O FOR a sculptor's hand,
That thou might'st take thy stand,
Thy wild hair floating on the eastern breeze,
Thy tranc'd yet open gaze
Fix'd on the desert haze,
As one who deep in heaven some airy pageant sees.

In outline dim and vast
Their fearful shadows cast
The giant forms of empires on their way
To ruin : one by one
They tower and they are gone,
Yet in the Prophet's soul the dreams of avarice stay.

No sun or star so bright
In all the world of light
That they should draw to heaven his downward eye :
He hears th' Almighty's word,
He sees the angel's sword,
Yet low upon the earth his heart and treasure lie.

Lo from yon argent field,
To him and us reveal'd,
One gentle star glides down, on earth to dwell.
Chain'd as they are below
Our eyes may see it glow,
And as it mounts again, may track its brightness well.

To him it glar'd afar,
A token of wild war,
The banner of his Lord's victorious wrath :
But close to us it gleams,
Its soothing lustre streams
Around our home's green walls, and on our church-
way path.

We in the tents abide
Which he at distance eyed
Like goodly cedars by the waters spread,
While seven red altar-fires
Rose up in wavy spires,
Where on the mount he watch'd his sorceries dark
and dread.

He watch'd till morning's ray
On lake and meadow lay,
And willow-shaded streams, that silent sweep
Around the banner'd lines,
Where by their several signs
The desert-wearied tribes in sight of Canaan sleep.

He watch'd till knowledge came
Upon his soul like flame,
Not of those magic fires at random caught :
But true prophetic light
Flash'd o'er him, high and bright,
Flash'd once, and died away, and left his darken'd
thought.

And can he choose but fear,
Who feels his God so near,
That when he fain would curse, his powerless tongue
In blessing only moves?—
Alas! the world he loves
Too close around his heart her tangling veil hath flung.

Sceptre and Star divine,
Who in thine inmost shrine
Hast made us worshippers, O claim thine own;
More than thy seers we know—
O teach our love to grow
Up to thy heavenly light, and reap what Thou hast
sown.

*A woman when she is in travail hath
sorrow, because her hour is come : but
as soon as she is delivered of the child,
she remembereth no more the anguish,
for joy that a man is born into the
world.* St. John xvi. 21.

W ELL may I guess and feel
   Why Autumn should be sad ;
But vernal airs should sorrow heal,
   Spring should be gay and glad :
Yet as along this violet bank I rove,
   The languid sweetness seems to choke my breath,
I sit me down beside the hazel grove,
And sigh, and half could wish my weariness were death.

   Like a bright veering cloud
      Grey blossoms twinkle there,
   Warbles around a busy crowd
      Of larks in purest air.
Shame on the heart that dreams of blessings gone,
   Or wakes the spectral forms of woe and crime,
When nature sings of joy and hope alone,
Reading her cheerful lesson in her own sweet time.

   Nor let the proud heart say,
      In her self-torturing hour,
   The travail pangs must have their way,
      The aching brow must lower.
To us long since the glorious Child is born,
   Our throes should be forgot, or only seem
Like a sad vision told for joy at morn,
For joy that we have wak'd and found it but a dream

Mysterious to all thought
A mother's prime of bliss,
When to her eager lips is brought
Her infant's thrilling kiss.
O never shall it set, the sacred light
Which dawns that moment on her tender gaze,
In the eternal distance blending bright
Her darling's hope and hers, for love and joy and praise.

No need for her to weep
Like Thracian wives of yore,
Save when in rapture still and deep
Her thankful heart runs o'er.
They mourn'd to trust their treasure on the main,
Sure of the storm, unknowing of their guide :
Welcome to her the peril and the pain,
For well she knows the home where they may safely
hide.

She joys that one is born
Into a world forgiven,
Her Father's household to adorn,
And dwell with her in heaven.
So have I seen, in spring's bewitching hour,
When the glad earth is offering all her best,
Some gentle maid bend o'er a cherish'd flower,
And wish it worthier on a Parent's heart to rest.

Nevertheless I tell you the truth; It is expedient for you that I go away; for if I go not away, the Comforter will not come unto you; but if I depart, I will send him unto you.
St. John xvi. 7.

M Y Saviour, can it ever be
   That I should gain by losing Thee?
The watchful mother tarries nigh
Though sleep have clos'd her infant's eye,
For should he wake, and find her gone,
She knows she could not bear his moan.
But I am weaker than a child,
   And Thou art more than mother dear;
Without Thee Heaven were but a wild:
   How can I live without Thee here!

"'Tis good for you, that I should go,
" You lingering yet awhile below;"—
'Tis thine own gracious promise, Lord!
Thy saints have prov'd the faithful word,
When Heaven's bright boundless avenue
Far open'd on their eager view,
And homeward to thy Father's throne,
   Still lessening, brightening on their sight,
Thy shadowy car went soaring on;
   They track'd Thee up th' abyss of light.

Thou bid'st rejoice; they dare not mourn,
But to their home in gladness turn,
Their home and God's, that favour'd place,
Where still he shines on Abraham's race,

In prayers and blessings there to wait
Like suppliants at their monarch's gate,
Who bent with bounty rare to aid
    The splendours of his crowning day,
Keeps back awhile his largess, made
    More welcome for that brief delay :

In doubt they wait, but not unblest ;
They doubt not of their Master's rest,
Nor of the gracious will of Heaven—
Who gave his Son, sure all has given—
But in ecstatic awe they muse
What course the genial stream may choose,
And far and wide their fancies rove,
    And to their height of wonder strain,
What secret miracle of love
    Should make their Saviour's going gain.

The days of hope and prayer are past,
The day of comfort dawns at last,
The everlasting gates again
Roll back, and, lo ! a royal train—
From the far depth of light once more
The floods of glory earth-ward pour :
They part like shower-drops in mid air,
    But ne'er so soft fell noon-tide shower,
Nor evening rain-bow gleam'd so fair
    To weary swains in parched bower.

Swiftly and straight each tongue of flame
Through cloud and breeze unwavering came,
And darted to its place of rest
On some meek brow of Jesus blest.
Nor fades it yet, that living gleam,
And still those lambent lightnings stream,
Where'er the Lord is, there are they ;
    In every heart that gives them room,

They light His altar every day,
  Zeal to inflame, and vice consume.

Soft as the plumes of Jesus' Dove
They nurse the soul to heavenly love:
The struggling spark of good within,
Just smother'd in the strife of sin,
They quicken to a timely glow,
The pure flame spreading high and low.
Said I, that prayer and hope were o'er?
  Nay, blessed Spirit! but by Thee
The Church's prayer finds wings to soar,
  The Church's hope finds eyes to see.

Then, fainting soul, arise and sing;
Mount, but be sober on the wing;
Mount up, for Heaven is won by prayer,
Be sober, for thou art not there;
Till Death the weary spirit free,
Thy God hath said, 'Tis good for thee
To walk by faith and not by sight:
  Take it on trust a little while;
Soon shalt thou read the mystery right
  In the full sunshine of His smile.

Or if thou yet more knowledge crave,
Ask thine own heart, that willing slave
To all that works thee woe or harm:
Shouldst thou not need some mighty charm
To win thee to thy Saviour's side,
Though He had deign'd with thee to bide?
The Spirit must stir the darkling deep,
  The Dove must settle on the Cross,
Else we should all sin on or sleep
  With Christ in sight, turning our gain to loss.

9

Fifth Sunday after Easter.

And the Lord was very angry with Aaron to have destroyed him: and I prayed for Aaron also the same time.
Deut. ix. 20.

ROGATION SUNDAY.

NOW is there solemn pause in earth and heaven;
  The Conqueror now
  His bonds hath riven,
And Angels wonder why he stays below:
  Yet hath not man his lesson learn'd,
  How endless love should be return'd.

Deep is the silence as of summer noon,
  When a soft shower
  Will trickle soon,
A gracious rain, freshening the weary bower—
  O sweetly then far off is heard
  The clear note of some lonely bird.

So let thy turtle dove's sad call arise
  In doubt and fear
  Through darkening·skies,
And pierce, O Lord, thy justly sealed ear,
  Where on the house top ᵐ, all night long,
  She trills her widow'd, faltering song.

Teach her to know and love her hour of prayer,
  And evermore,
  As faith grows rare,
Unlock her heart, and offer all its store
  In holier love and humbler vows,
  As suits a lost returning spouse.

   ᵐ Psalm cii. 7

Not as at first [n], but with intenser cry,
     Upon the mount
     She now must lie,
Till thy dear love to blot the sad account
     Of her rebellious race be won,
     Pitying the mother in the son.

But chiefly, for she knows thee anger'd worst
     By holiest things
     Profan'd and curst,
Chiefly for Aaron's seed she spreads her wings,
     If but one leaf she may from Thee
     Win of the reconciling tree.

For what shall heal, when holy water banes?
     Or who may guide
     O'er desert plains
Thy lov'd yet sinful people wandering wide,
     If Aaron's hand unshrinking mould [o]
     An idol form of earthly gold?

Therefore her tears are bitter, and as deep
     Her boding sigh,
     As, while men sleep,
Sad hearted mothers heave, that wakeful lie,
     To muse upon some darling child
     Roaming in youth's uncertain wild.

Therefore on fearful dreams her inward sight
     Is fain to dwell—
     What lurid light
Shall the last darkness of the world dispel,
     The Mediator in his wrath
     Descending down the lightning's path.

[n] I fell down before the Lord forty days and forty nights, as I fell
down at the first. *Deuteronomy* ix. 25.   [o] Exodus xxxii. 4.

Yet, yet awhile, offended Saviour, pause,
    In act to break P
    Thine outrag'd laws,
O spare thy rebels for thine own dear sake ;
    Withdraw thine hand, nor dash to earth
    The covenant of our second birth.

'Tis forfeit like the first—we own it all—
    Yet for love's sake,
    Let it not fall ;
But at thy touch let veiled hearts awake,
    That nearest to thine altar lie,
    Yet least of holy things descry.

Teacher of teachers ! Priest of priests ! from Thee
    The sweet strong prayer
    Must rise, to free
First Levi, then all Israel, from the snare.
    Thou art our Moses out of sight—
    Speak for us, or we perish quite.

P Exodus xxxii. 19.

Ascension Day.

*Why stand ye gazing up into heaven?
this same Jesus, which is taken up
from you into heaven, shall so come
in like manner as ye have seen him
go into heaven.* Acts i. 11.

SOFT cloud, that while the breeze of May
   Chants her glad matins in the leafy arch,
Draw'st thy bright veil across the heavenly way,
Meet pavement for an angel's glorious march :

   My soul is envious of mine eye,
That it should soar and glide with thee so fast,
   The while my groveling thoughts half buried lie,
Or lawless roam around this earthly waste.

   Chains of my heart, avaunt I say—
I will arise, and in the strength of love
   Pursue the bright track ere it fade away,
My Saviour's pathway to his home above.

   Sure, when I reach the point where earth
Melts into nothing from th' uncumber'd sight,
   Heaven will o'ercome th' attraction of my birth,
And I shall sink in yonder sea of light :

   Till resting by th' incarnate Lord,
Once bleeding, now triumphant for my sake,
   I mark him, how by seraph hosts ador'd
He to earth's lowest cares is still awake.

   The sun and every vassal star,
All space, beyond the soar of Angel wings,

Wait on His word : and yet he stays his car
For every sigh a contrite suppliant brings.

He listens to the silent tear
For all the anthems of the boundless sky—
    And shall our dreams of music bar our ear
To His soul-piercing voice for ever nigh ?

Nay, gracious Saviour—but as now
Our thoughts have trac'd thee to thy glory-throne,
    So help us evermore with thee to bow
Where human sorrow breathes her lowly moan.

We must not stand to gaze too long,
Though on unfolding Heaven our gaze we bend,
    Where lost behind the bright angelic throng
We see Christ's entering triumph slow ascend.

No fear but we shall soon behold,
Faster than now it fades, that gleam revive,
    When issuing from his cloud of fiery gold
Our wasted frames feel the true sun, and live.

Then shall we see Thee as Thou art,
For ever fix'd in no unfruitful gaze,
    But such as lifts the new-created heart,
Age after age, in worthier love and praise.

Sunday after Ascension.

As every man hath received the gift, even so minister the same one to another, as good stewards of the manifold grace of God. 1 St. Peter iv. 10.

THE Earth that in her genial breast
　　Makes for the down a kindly nest,
Where wafted by the warm south-west
　　　　It floats at pleasure,
Yields, thankful, of her very best,
　　　　To nurse her treasure :

True to her trust, tree, herb, or reed,
She renders for each scatter'd seed,
And to her Lord with duteous heed
　　　　Gives large increase :
Thus year by year she works unfeed,
　　　　And will not cease.

Woe worth these barren hearts of ours,
Where Thou hast set celestial flowers,
And water'd with more balmy showers,
　　　　Than e'er distill'd
In Eden, on th' ambrosial bowers—
　　　　Yet nought we yield.

Largely Thou givest, gracious Lord,
Largely thy gifts should be restor'd ;
Freely Thou givest, and thy word
　　　　Is, " freely give q."
He only, who forgets to hoard,
　　　　Has learn'd to live.

q St. Matthew x. 8.

Wisely Thou givest—all around
Thine equal rays are resting found,
Yet varying so on various ground
　　　　They pierce and strike,
That not two roseate cups are crown'd
　　　　With dew alike :

Even so, in silence, likest Thee,
Steals on soft-handed Charity,
Tempering her gifts, that seem so free,
　　　　By time and place,
Till not a woe the bleak world see,
　　　　But finds her grace :

Eyes to the blind, and to the lame
Feet, and to sinners wholesome blame,
To starving bodies food and flame
　　　　By turns she brings,
To humbled souls, that sink for shame,
　　　　Lends heaven-ward wings :

Leads them the way our Saviour went,
And shews Love's treasure yet unspent ;
As when th' unclouded heavens were rent
　　　　Opening his road,
Nor yet his Holy Spirit sent
　　　　To our abode.

Ten days th' eternal doors display'd
Were wondering, so th' Almighty bade,
Whom Love enthron'd would send, in aid
　　　　Of souls that mourn,
Left orphans in Earth's dreary shade
　　　　As soon as born.

Open they stand, that prayers in throngs
May rise on high, and holy songs,

Such incense as of right belongs
      To the true shrine,
Where stands the Healer of all wrongs
      In light divine ;

The golden censer in his hand,
He offers hearts from every land,
Tied to his own by gentlest band
      Of silent Love :
About Him winged blessings stand
      In act to move.

A little while, and they shall fleet
From Heaven to Earth, attendants meet
On the life-giving Paraclete
      Speeding his flight,
With all that sacred is and sweet,
      On saints to light.

Apostles, Prophets, Pastors, all
Shall feel the shower of Mercy fall,
And starting at th' Almighty's call,
      Give what He gave,
Till their high deeds the world appal,
      And sinners save.

Whitsunday.

WHEN God of old came down from Heaven,
    In power and wrath he came ;
Before his feet the clouds were riven,
    Half darkness and half flame :

Around the trembling mountain's base
    The prostrate people lay,
Convinc'd of sin, but not of grace ;
    It was a dreadful day.

But when He came the second time,
    He came in power and love,
Softer than gale at morning prime
    Hover'd his holy Dove.

The fires that rush'd on Sinai down
    In sudden torrents dread,
Now gently light, a glorious crown,
    On every sainted head.

Like arrows went those lightnings forth
    Wing'd with the sinner's doom,
But these, like tongues, o'er all the earth
    Proclaiming life to come :

And as on Israel's awe-struck ear
    The voice exceeding loud,

The trump, that angels quake to hear,
    Thrill'd from the deep, dark cloud,

So, when the Spirit of our God
    Came down his flock to find,
A voice from heaven was heard abroad,
    A rushing, mighty wind.

Nor doth the outward ear alone
    At that high warning start ;
Conscience gives back th' appalling tone ;
    'Tis echoed in the heart.

It fills the Church of God ; it fills
    The sinful world around ;
Only in stubborn hearts and wills
    No place for it is found.

To other strains our souls are set :
    A giddy whirl of sin
Fills ear and brain, and will not let
    Heaven's harmonies come in.

Come Lord, come Wisdom, Love, and Power,
    Open our ears to hear ;
Let us not miss th' accepted hour ;
    Save, Lord, by Love or Fear.

Monday in Whitsun-week.

So the Lord scattered them abroad from thence upon the face of all the earth: and they left off to build the city.
Genesis xi. 8.

SINCE all that is not heav'n must fade,
　Light be the hand of Ruin laid
　　Upon the home I love :
With lulling spell let soft Decay
Steal on, and spare the giant sway,
　　The crash of tower and grove.

Far opening down some woodland deep
In their own quiet glade should sleep
　　The relics dear to thought,
And wild-flower wreaths from side to side
Their waving tracery hang, to hide
　　What ruthless Time has wrought.

Such are the visions green and sweet
That o'er the wistful fancy fleet
　　In Asia's sea-like plain,
Where slowly, round his isles of sand,
Euphrates through the lonely land
　　Winds toward the pearly main.

Slumber is there, but not of rest ;
There her forlorn and weary nest
　　The famish'd hawk has found,
The wild dog howls at fall of night,
The serpent's rustling coils affright
　　The traveller on his round.

What shapeless form, half lost on-high [r],
Half seen against the evening sky,
　　Seems like a ghost to glide,
And watch, from Babel's crumbling heap,
Where in her shadow, fast asleep,
　　Lies fall'n imperial Pride?

With half-clos'd eye a lion there
Is basking in his noontide lair,
　　Or prowls in twilight gloom.
The golden city's king he seems,
Such as in old prophetic dreams [s]
　　Sprang from rough ocean's womb.

But where are now his eagle wings,
That shelter'd erst a thousand kings,
　　Hiding the glorious sky
From half the nations, till they own
No holier name, no mightier throne?
　　That vision is gone by.

Quench'd is the golden statue's ray [t],
The breath of heaven has blown away
　　What toiling earth had pil'd,
Scattering wise heart and crafty hand,
As breezes strew on ocean's sand
　　The fabrics of a child.

Divided thence through every age
Thy rebels, Lord, their warfare wage,

[r] See Sir R. K. Porter's Travels, ii. 387. "In my second visit
to Birs Nimrood, my party suddenly halted, having descried several
dark objects moving along the summit of its hill, which they con-
strued into dismounted Arabs on the look out : I took out my glass
to examine, and soon distinguished that the causes of our alarm
were two or three majestic lions, taking the air upon the heights of
the pyramid.　　　[s] Daniel vii. 4.　　　[t] Daniel ii. and iii.

And hoarse and jarring all
Mount up their heaven assailing cries
To thy bright watchmen in the skies
From Babel's shatter'd wall.

Thrice only since, with blended might
The nations on that haughty height
Have met to scale the heaven :
Thrice only might a Seraph's look
A moment's shade of sadness brook—
Such power to guilt was given.

Now the fierce Bear and Leopard keen [u]
Are perish'd as they ne'er had been,
Oblivion is their home :
Ambition's boldest dream and last
Must melt before the clarion blast
That sounds the dirge of Rome.

Heroes and Kings, obey the charm,
Withdraw the proud high-reaching arm,
There is an oath on high,
That ne'er on brow of mortal birth
Shall blend again the crowns of earth,
Nor in according cry

Her many voices mingling own
One tyrant Lord, one idol throne :
But to His triumph soon
He shall descend, who rules above,
And the pure language of His love [v]
All tongues of men shall tune.

[u] Daniel vii. 5, 6.

[v] Then will I turn to the people a pure language, that they may all call upon the name of the Lord, to serve him with one consent. *Zephaniah* iii. 9.

Nor let Ambition heartless mourn ;
When Babel's very ruins burn,
 Her high desires may breathe ;—
O'ercome thyself, and thou may'st share
With Christ his Father's throne [x], and wear
 The world's imperial wreath.

[x] To him that overcometh will I grant to sit with me in my throne. *Revelations* iii. 21.

Addressed to Candidates for Ordination.

" LORD, in thy field I work all day,
   " I read, I teach, I warn, I pray,
" And yet these wilful wandering sheep
" Within thy fold I cannot keep.

" I journey, yet no step is won—
" Alas ! the weary course I run !
" Like sailors shipwreck'd in their dreams,
" All powerless and benighted seems."

What? wearied out with half a life?
Scar'd with this smooth unbloody strife ?
Think where thy coward hopes had flown
Had Heaven held out the martyr's crown.

How could'st thou hang upon the cross,
To whom a weary hour is loss ?
Or how the thorns and scourging brook,
Who shrinkest from a scornful look ?

Yet ere thy craven spirit faints,
Hear thine own King, the King of saints ;
Though thou wert toiling in the grave,
'Tis He can cheer thee, He can save.

He is th' eternal mirror bright,
Where angels view the Father's light,
And yet in Him the simplest swain
May read his homely lesson plain.

Early to quit his home on earth,
And claim his high celestial birth,
Alone with his true Father found
Within the temple's solemn round :—

Yet in meek duty to abide
For many a year at Mary's side,
Nor heed, though restless spirits ask,
"What? hath the Christ forgot his task?"—

Conscious of Deity within,
To bow before an heir of sin,
With folded arms on humble breast,
By his own servant wash'd and blest :—

Then full of Heaven, the mystic Dove
Hovering his gracious brow above,
To shun the voice and eye of praise,
And in the wild his trophies raise :—

With hymns of angels in his ears,
Back to his task of woe and tears,
Unmurmuring through the world to roam
With not a wish or thought at home :—

All but himself to heal and save,
Till ripen'd for the cross and grave
He to His Father gently yield
The breath that our redemption seal'd :—

Then to unearthly life arise,
Yet not at once to seek the skies,
But glide awhile from saint to saint,
Lest on our lonely way we faint ;

And through the cloud by glimpses shew
How bright, in Heaven, the marks will glow

10

Of the true cross, imprinted deep
Both on the Shepherd and the sheep :—

When out of sight, in heart and prayer
Thy chosen people still to bear,
And from behind thy glorious veil,
Shed light that cannot change or fail :—

This is thy pastoral course, O Lord,
Till we be sav'd, and Thou ador'd ;—
Thy course and ours—but who are they
Who follow on the narrow way ?

And yet of Thee from year to year
The Church's solemn chant we hear,
As from thy cradle to thy throne
She swells her high heart-cheering tone.

Listen, ye pure white-robed souls,
Whom in her list she now enrolls,
And gird ye for your high emprize
By these her thrilling minstrelsies.

And wheresoe'er, in earth's wide field,
Ye lift, for Him, the red-cross shield,
Be this your song, your joy and pride—
" Our Champion went before and died."

𝕿rinity 𝕾unday.

If I have told you earthly things, and ye believe not, how shall ye believe, if I tell you of heavenly things? St. John iii. 12.

C REATOR, Saviour, strengthening Guide,
  Now on Thy mercy's ocean wide
Far out of sight we seem to glide.

Help us, each hour, with steadier eye
To search the deepening mystery,
The wonders of Thy sea and sky.

The blessed angels look and long
To praise Thee with a worthier song,
And yet our silence does Thee wrong.

Along the Church's central space
The sacred weeks with unfelt pace
Have borne us on from grace to grace.

As travellers on some woodland height,
When wintry suns are gleaming bright,
Lose in arch'd glades their tangled sight ;—

By glimpses such as dreamers love
Through her grey veil the leafless grove
Shews where the distant shadows rove ;—

Such trembling joy the soul o'er-awes
As nearer to thy shrine she draws :—
And now before the choir we pause.

The door is clos'd—but soft and deep
Around the awful arches sweep
Such airs as soothe a hermit's sleep.

From each carv'd nook and fretted bend
Cornice and gallery seem to send
Tones that with seraph hymns might blend.

Three solemn parts together twine
In harmony's mysterious line ;
Three solemn aisles approach the shrine :

Yet all are One—together all,
In thoughts that awe but not appal,
Teach the adoring heart to fall.

Within these walls each fluttering guest
Is gently lur'd to one safe nest—
Without, 'tis moaning and unrest.

The busy world a thousand ways
Is hurrying by, nor ever stays
To catch a note of Thy dear praise.

Why tarries not her chariot wheel,
That o'er her with no vain appeal
One gust of heavenly song might steal ?

Alas ! for her Thy opening flowers
Unheeded breathe to summer showers,
Unheard the music of Thy bowers.

What echoes from the sacred dome
The selfish spirit may o'ercome
That will not hear of love or home ?

The heart that scorn'd a father's care
How can it rise in filial prayer ?
How an all-seeing Guardian bear ?

Or how shall envious brethren own
A Brother on th' eternal throne,
Their Father's joy, their hope alone?

How shall thy Spirit's gracious wile
The sullen brow of gloom beguile,
That frowns on sweet affection's smile?

Eternal One, Almighty Trine!
Since Thou art ours, and we are Thine,
By all thy love did once resign,

By all the grace thy heavens still hide,
We pray thee, keep us at thy side,
Creator, Saviour, strengthening Guide!

First Sunday after Trinity.

So Joshua smote all the country . . . and all their kings: he left none remaining. Joshua x. 40.

WHERE is the land with milk and honey flowing,
 The promise of our God, our fancy's theme?
Here over shatter'd walls dank weeds are growing,
 And blood and fire have run in mingled stream;
  Like oaks and cedars all around
  The giant corses strew the ground,
And haughty Jericho's cloud-piercing wall
Lies where it sank at Joshua's trumpet call.

These are not scenes for pastoral dance at even,
 For moonlight rovings in the fragrant glades,
Soft slumbers in the open eye of heaven,
 And all the listless joy of summer shades.
  We in the midst of ruins live,
  Which every hour dread warning give,
Nor may our household vine or fig tree hide
The broken arches of old Canaan's pride.

Where is the sweet repose of hearts repenting,
 The deep calm sky, the sunshine of the soul,
Now heaven and earth are to our bliss consenting,
 And all the Godhead joins to make us whole?
  The triple crown of mercy now
  Is ready for the suppliant's brow,
By the Almighty Three for ever plann'd,
And from behind the cloud held out by Jesus' hand.

 " Now, Christians, hold your own—the land before ye
 " Is open—win your way, and take your rest."

So sounds our war-note ; but our path of glory
  By many a cloud is darken'd and unblest :
    And daily as we downward glide,
    Life's ebbing stream on either side
Shews at each turn some mouldering hope or joy.
The Man seems following still the funeral of the Boy.

Open our eyes, thou Sun of life and gladness,
  That we may see that glorious world of thine !
It shines for us in vain, while drooping sadness
    Enfolds us here like mist : come Power benign
      Touch our chill'd hearts with vernal smile,
      Our wintry course do Thou beguile,
Not by the wayside ruins let us mourn,
Who have th' eternal towers for our appointed bourne.

Second Sunday after Trinity.

Marvel not, my brethren, if the world hate you. We know that we have passed from death unto life, because we love the brethren. 1 John iii. 13, 14.

THE clouds that wrap the setting sun
    When Autumn's softest gleams are ending,
Where all bright hues together run
    In sweet confusion blending :—
Why, as we watch their floating wreath,
Seem they the breath of life to breathe?
To Fancy's eye their motions prove
They mantle round the Sun for love.

When up some woodland dale we catch
    The many-twinkling smile ʸ of ocean,
Or with pleas'd ear bewilder'd watch
    His chime of restless motion ;
Still as the surging waves retire
They seem to gasp with strong desire,
Such signs of love old Ocean gives,
We cannot choose but think he lives.

Wouldst thou the life of souls discern?
    Nor human wisdom nor divine
Helps thee by aught beside to learn ;
    Love is life's only sign.
The spring of the regenerate heart,
The pulse, the glow of every part,
Is the true love of Christ our Lord,
As man embrac'd, as God ador'd.

ʸ . . . . πoντίων τε κυμάτων
ἀνήριθμον γέλασμα. . . . . Æschyl. Prom. 89.

But he, whose heart will bound to mark
  The full bright burst of summer morn,
Loves too each little dewy spark
    By leaf or flow'ret worn :
Cheap forms, and common hues, 'tis true,
Through the bright shower-drop meet his view ;
The colouring may be of this earth ;
The lustre comes of heavenly birth.

Even so, who loves the Lord aright,
  No soul of man can worthless find ;
All will be precious in his sight,
    Since Christ on all hath shin'd :
But chiefly Christian souls ; for they,
Though worn and soil'd with sinful clay,
Are yet, to eyes that see them true,
All glistening with baptismal dew.

Then marvel not, if such as bask
  In purest light of innocence,
Hope against hope, in love's dear task,
    Spite of all dark offence.
If they who hate the trespass most,
Yet, when all other love is lost,
Love the poor sinner, marvel not ;
Christ's mark outwears the rankest blot.

No distance breaks the tie of blood ;
  Brothers are brothers evermore ;
Nor wrong, nor wrath of deadliest mood,
    That magic may o'erpower ;
Oft, ere the common source be known,
The kindred drops will claim their own,
And throbbing pulses silently
Move heart towards heart by sympathy.

So is it with true Christian hearts ;
  Their mutual share in Jesus' blood

An everlasting bond imparts
    Of holiest brotherhood :
Oh ! might we all our lineage prove,
Give and forgive, do good and love,
By soft endearments in kind strife
Lightening the load of daily life !

There is much need : for not as yet
    Are we in shelter or repose,
The holy house is still beset
    With leaguer of stern foes ;
Wild thoughts within, bad men without,
All evil spirits round about,
Are banded in unblest device,
To spoil Love's earthly paradise.

Then draw we nearer day by day,
    Each to his brethren, all to God ;
Let the world take us as she may,
    We must not change our road ;
Not wondering, though in grief, to find
The martyr's foe still keep her mind ;
But fix'd to hold Love's banner fast,
And by submission win at last.

Third Sunday after Trinity.

There is joy in the presence of the angels of God over one sinner that repenteth. St. Luke xv. 10.

O HATEFUL spell of Sin! when friends are nigh,
  To make stern Memory tell her tale unsought,
And raise accusing shades of hours gone by,
  To come between us and all kindly thought!

Chill'd at her touch, the self-reproaching soul
  Flies from the heart and home she dearest loves
To where lone mountains tower, or billows roll,
  Or to your endless depth, ye solemn groves.

In vain: the averted cheek in loneliest dell
  Is conscious of a gaze it cannot bear,
The leaves that rustle near us seem to tell
  Our heart's sad secret to the silent air.

Nor is the dream untrue: for all around
  The heavens are watching with their thousand eyes,
We cannot pass our guardian angel's bound,
  Resign'd or sullen, he will hear our sighs.

He in the mazes of the budding wood
  Is near, and mourns to see our thankless glance
Dwell coldly, where the fresh green earth is strew'd
  With the first flowers that lead the vernal dance.

In wasteful bounty shower'd, they smile unseen,
  Unseen by man—but what if purer sprights
By moonlight o'er their dewy bosoms lean
  To' adore the Father of all gentle lights?

If such there be, O grief and shame to think
   That sight of thee should overcloud their joy,
A new born soul, just waiting on the brink
   Of endless life, yet wrapt in earth's annoy !

O turn, and be thou turn'd ! the selfish tear,
   In bitter thoughts of low born care begun,
Let it flow on, but flow refin'd and clear,
   The turbid waters brightening as they run.

Let it flow on, till all thine earthly heart
   In penitential drops have ebb'd away,
Then fearless turn where Heaven hath set thy part,
   Nor shudder at the eye that saw thee stray.

O lost and found ! all gentle souls below
   Their dearest welcome shall prepare, and prove
Such joy o'er thee, as raptur'd seraphs know,
   Who learn their lesson at the Throne of Love.

Fourth Sunday after Trinity.

I T was not then a poet's dream,
  An idle vaunt of song,
Such as beneath the moon's soft gleam
  On vacant fancies throng;

Which bids us see in heaven and earth,
  In all fair things around,
Strong yearnings for a blest new birth
  With sinless glories crown'd;

Which bids us hear, at each sweet pause
  From care and want and toil,
When dewy eve her curtain draws
  Over the day's turmoil,

In the low chant of wakeful birds,
  In the deep weltering flood,
In whispering leaves, these solemn words—
  "God made us all for good."

All true, all faultless, all in tune,
　　Creation's wondrous choir
Open'd in mystic unison
　　To last till time expire.

And still it lasts : by day and night,
　　With one consenting voice,
All hymn thy glory, Lord, aright,
　　All worship and rejoice.

Man only mars the sweet accord,
　　O'erpowering with " harsh din "
The music of thy works and word,
　　Ill match'd with grief and sin.

Sin is with man at morning break,
　　And through the live-long day
Deafens the ear that fain would wake
　　To Nature's simple lay.

But when eve's silent foot-fall steals
　　Along the eastern sky,
And one by one to earth reveals
　　Those purer fires on high,

When one by one each human sound
　　Dies on the awful ear,
Then Nature's voice no more is drown'd,
　　She speaks and we must hear.

Then pours she on the Christian heart
　　That warning still and deep,
At which high spirits of old would start
　　E'en from their Pagan sleep,

Just guessing, through their murky blind,
　　Few, faint, and baffling sight,

Streaks of a brighter heaven behind,
  A cloudless depth of light.

Such thoughts, the wreck of Paradise,
  Through many a dreary age,
Upbore whate'er of good and wise
  Yet lived in bard or sage :

They mark'd what agonizing throes
  Shook the great mother's womb ;
But Reason's spells might not disclose
  The gracious birth to come ;

Nor could th' enchantress Hope forecast
  God's secret love and power ;
The travail pangs of Earth must last
  Till her appointed hour ;

The hour that saw from opening heaven
  Redeeming glory stream,
Beyond the summer hues of even,
  Beyond the mid-day beam.

Thenceforth, to eyes of high desire,
  The meanest things below,
As with a seraph's robe of fire
  Invested, burn and glow :

The rod of heaven has touch'd them, all,
  The word from heaven is spoken ;
" Rise, shine, and sing, thou captive thrall ;
  " Are not thy fetters broken ?

" The God who hallow'd thee and blest,
  " Pronouncing thee all good—
" Hath He not all thy wrongs redrest,
  " And all thy bliss renew'd ?

" Why mourn'st thou still as one bereft,
" Now that th' eternal Son
" His blessed home in heaven hath left
" To make thee all his own ? "

Thou mourn'st because Sin lingers still
    In Christ's new heaven and earth ;
Because our rebel works and will
    Stain our immortal birth :

Because, as Love and Prayer grow cold,
    The Saviour hides his face,
And worldlings blot the temple's gold
    With uses vile and base.

Hence all thy groans and travail pains,
    Hence, till thy God return,
In wisdom's ear thy blithest strains,
    Oh Nature, seem to mourn.

Fifth Sunday after Trinity.

And Simon answering said unto him,
Master, we have toiled all the night,
and have taken nothing: nevertheless
at thy word I will let down the net.
And when they had this done, they
inclosed a great multitude of fishes:
and their net brake. St. Luke v. 5, 6.

" THE live long night we've toil'd in vain,
   " But at thy gracious word
" I will let down the net again :—
   " Do thou thy will, O Lord !"

So spake the weary fisher, spent
   With bootless darkling toil,
Yet on his Master's bidding bent
   For love and not for spoil.

So day by day and week by week,
   In sad and weary thought,
They muse, whom God hath set to seek
   The souls his Christ hath bought.

For not upon a tranquil lake
   Our pleasant task we ply,
Where all along our glistening wake
   The softest moonbeams lie ;

Where rippling wave and dashing oar
   Our midnight chant attend,
Or whispering palm-leaves from the shore
   With midnight silence blend.

Sweet thoughts of peace, ye may not last :
   Too soon some ruder sound

11

Calls us from where ye soar so fast
    Back to our earthly round.

For wildest storms our ocean sweep :—
    No anchor but the Cross
Might hold : and oft the thankless deep
    Turns all our toil to loss.

Full many a dreary anxious hour
    We watch our nets alone
In drenching spray, and driving shower,
    And hear the night-bird's moan :

At morn we look, and nought is there ;
    Sad dawn of cheerless day !
Who then from pining and despair
    The sickening heart can stay ?

There is a stay—and we are strong ;
    Our Master is at hand,
To cheer our solitary song,
    And guide us to the strand,

In his own time : but yet awhile
    Our bark at sea must ride :
Cast after cast, by force or guile
    All waters must be tried :

By blameless guile or gentle force,
    As when He deign'd to teach—
The lode-star of our Christian course—
    Upon this sacred beach.

Should e'er thy wonder-working grace
    Triumph by our weak arm,
Let not our sinful fancy trace
    Aught human in the charm :

To our own nets [z] ne'er bow we down,
    Lest on the eternal shore
The angels, while our draught they own [a],
    Reject us evermore :

Or, if for our unworthiness
    Toil, prayer, and watching fail,
In disappointment Thou canst bless,
    So love at heart prevail.

[z] They sacrifice unto their net, and burn incense unto their drag. *Habakkuk* i. 16.   [a] St. Matthew xiii. 49.

Sixth Sunday after Trinity.

David said unto Nathan, I have sinned against the Lord. And Nathan said unto David, The Lord also hath put away thy sin; thou shalt not die.
2 Samuel xii. 13.

WHEN bitter thoughts, of conscience born,
　　With sinners wake at morn,
When from our restless couch we start,
With fever'd lips and wither'd heart,
Where is the spell to charm those mists away,
And make new morning in that darksome day?
　　One draught of spring's delicious air,
　　One stedfast thought, that God is there.

These are thy wonders, hourly wrought [b],
　　Thou Lord of time and thought,
Lifting and lowering souls at will,
Crowding a world of good or ill
Into a moment's vision : even as light
Mounts o'er a cloudy ridge, and all is bright,
　　From west to east one thrilling ray
　　Turning a wintry world to May.

Wouldst thou the pangs of guilt assuage?
　　Lo here an open page,
Where heavenly mercy shines as free,
Written in balm, sad heart, for thee.

[b] See Herbert's Poems, p. 160.

Never so fast, in silent April shower,
Flush'd into green the dry and leafless bower [c],
    As Israel's crowned mourner felt
    The dull hard stone within him melt.

    The absolver saw the mighty grief,
        And hasten'd with relief ;—
    " The Lord forgives ; thou shalt not die : "—
    'Twas gently spoke, yet heard on high,
And all the band of angels, us'd to sing
In heaven, according to his raptur'd string,
    Who many a month had turn'd away
    With veiled eyes, nor own'd his lay,

    Now spread their wings, and throng around
        To the glad mournful sound,
    And welcome, with bright open face,
    The broken heart to love's embrace.
The rock is smitten, and to future years
Springs ever fresh the tide of holy tears [d]
    And holy music, whispering peace
    Till time and sin together cease.

    There drink : and when ye are at rest,
        With that free Spirit blest [e],
    Who to the contrite can dispense
    The princely heart of innocence,
If ever, floating from faint earthly lyre,
Was wafted to your soul one high desire,

      [c] And all this leafless and uncolour'd scene
        Shall flush into variety again. *Cowper.*

[d] Psalm xxi.

[e] Psalm li. 12. " Uphold me with thy free spirit." The original
word seems to mean " ingenuous, princely, noble." Read Bishop
Horne's Paraphrase on the verse.

By all the trembling hope ye feel,
Think on the minstrel as ye kneel :

Think on the shame, that dreadful hour
    When tears shall have no power,
Should his own lay th' accuser prove,
Cold while he kindled others' love :
And let your prayer for charity arise,
That his own heart may hear his melodies,
    And a true voice to him may cry,
    " Thy God forgives—thou shalt not die."

Seventh Sunday *From whence can a man satisfy these*
after Trinity. *men with bread here in the wilderness?*
St. Mark viii. 4.

G O not away, thou weary soul :
  Heaven has in store a precious dole
Here on Bethsaida's cold and darksome height,
  Where over rocks and sands arise
  Proud Sirion in the northern skies,
And Tabor's lonely peak, 'twixt thee and noon-day light.

  And far below, Gennesaret's main
  Spreads many a mile of liquid plain,
Though all seem gather'd in one eager bound,
  Then narrowing cleaves yon palmy lea,
  Towards that deep sulphureous sea,
Where five proud cities lie, by one dire sentence drown'd.

  Landscape of fear ! yet, weary heart,
  Thou needst not in thy gloom depart,
Nor fainting turn to seek thy distant home :
  Sweetly thy sickening throbs are ey'd
  By the kind Saviour at thy side ;
For healing and for balm even now thine hour is come.

  No fiery wing is seen to glide,
  No cates ambrosial are supplied,
But one poor fisher's rude and scanty store
  Is all He asks, and more than needs,
  Who men and angels daily feeds,
And stills the wailing sea-bird on the hungry shore.

  The feast is o'er, the guests are gone,
  And over all that upland lone

The breeze of eve sweeps wildly as of old—
 But far unlike the former dreams,
 The heart's sweet moonlight softly gleams
Upon life's varied view, so joyless erst and cold

 As mountain travellers in the night,
 When heaven by fits is dark and bright,
Pause listening on the silent heath, and hear
 Nor trampling hoof nor tinkling bell,
 Then bolder scale the rugged fell,
Conscious the more of One, ne'er seen, yet ever near :

 So when the tones of rapture gay
 On the lorn ear, die quite away,
The lonely world seems lifted nearer heaven ;
 Seen daily, yet unmark'd before,
 Earth's common paths are strewn all o'er
With flowers of pensive hope, the wreath of man forgiven.

 The low sweet tones of Nature's lyre
 No more on listless ears expire,
Nor vainly smiles along the shady way
 The primrose in her vernal nest,
 Nor unlamented sink to rest
Sweet roses one by one, nor autumn leaves decay.

 There's not a star the heaven can shew,
 There's not a cottage hearth below,
But feeds with solace kind the willing soul—
 Men love us, or they need our love ;
 Freely they own, or heedless prove
The curse of lawless hearts, the joy of self-control.

 Then rouse thee from desponding sleep,
 Nor by the wayside lingering weep,
Nor fear to seek Him farther in the wild,
 Whose love can turn earth's worst and least
 Into a conqueror's royal feast :
Thou wilt not be untrue, thou shalt not be beguil'd.

Eighth Sunday after Trinity. *It is the man of God, who was disobedient unto the word of the Lord.* 1 Kings xiii. 26.

PROPHET of God, arise and take
　　With thee the words of wrath divine,
　　The scourge of Heaven, to shake
　　O'er yon apostate shrine.

Where angels down the lucid stair
Came hovering to our sainted sires,
　　Now, in the twilight, glare
　　The heathen's wizard fires.

Go, with thy voice the altar rend,
Scatter the ashes, be the arm,
　　That idols would befriend,
　　Shrunk at thy withering charm.

Then turn thee, for thy time is short,
But trace not o'er the former way,
　　Lest idol pleasures court
　　Thy heedless soul astray.

Thou know'st how hard to hurry by,
Where on the lonely woodland road
　　Beneath the moonlight sky
　　The festal warblings flow'd ;

Where maidens to the Queen of Heaven
Wove the gay dance round oak or palm,
　　Or breath'd their vows at even
　　In hymns as soft as balm.

Or thee perchance a darker spell
Enthralls : the smooth stones of the flood [f],
    By mountain grot or fell,
    Pollute with infant's blood ;

The giant altar on the rock,
The cavern whence the timbrel's call
    Affrights the wandering flock :—
    Thou long'st to search them all.

Trust not the dangerous path again—
O forward step and lingering will !
    O lov'd and warn'd in vain !
    And wilt thou perish still ?

Thy message given, thine home in sight,
To the forbidden feast return ?
    Yield to the false delight
    Thy better soul could spurn ?

Alas, my brother ! round thy tomb
In sorrow kneeling, and in fear,
    We read the Pastor's doom
    Who speaks and will not hear.

The grey-hair'd saint may fail at last,
The surest guide a wanderer prove ;
    Death only binds us fast
    To the bright shore of love.

[f] Among the smooth stones of the stream is thy portion ; they, they are thy lot. *Isaiah* lvii. 6.

Ninth Sunday after Trinity.

And after the earthquake a fire; but the Lord was not in the fire: and after the fire a still small voice. 1 Kings xix. 12.

IN troublous days of anguish and rebuke,
  While sadly round them Israel's children look,
And their eyes fail for waiting on their Lord :
While underneath each awful arch of green,
On every mountain top, God's chosen scene
  Of pure heart-worship, Baal is ador'd :

'Tis well, true hearts should for a time retire
To holy ground, in quiet to aspire
  Towards promis'd regions of serener grace ;
On Horeb, with Elijah, let us lie,
Where all around on mountain, sand, and sky,
  God's chariot-wheels have left distinctest trace :

There, if in jealousy and strong disdain
We to the sinner's God of sin complain,
  Untimely seeking here the peace of heaven—
" It is enough, O Lord ! now let me die
" Even as my fathers did : for what am I
  " That I should stand, where they have vainly
    " striven ? "—

Perhaps our God may of our conscience ask,
" What doest thou here, frail wanderer from thy
    " task ?
  " Where hast thou left those few sheep in the
    wild *? "

ᵍ 1 Samuel xvii. 28.

Then should we plead our heart's consuming pain,
At sight of ruin'd altars, prophets slain,
   And God's own ark with blood of souls defil'd ;

He on the rock may bid us stand, and see
The outskirts of his march of mystery,
   His endless warfare with man's wilful heart ;
First, His great Power He to the sinner shows,
Lo ! at His angry blast the rocks unclose,
   And to their base the trembling mountains part :

Yet the Lord is not here : 'tis not by Power
He will be known—but 'darker tempests lower ;
   Still, sullen heavings vex the labouring ground :
Perhaps His Presence thro' all depth and height,
Best of all gems, that deck his crown of light,
   The haughty eye may dazzle and confound.

God is not in the earthquake ; but behold
From Sinai's caves are bursting, as of old,
   The flames of His consuming jealous ire.
Woe to the sinner, should stern Justice prove
His chosen attribute ;—but He in love
   Hastes to proclaim, " God is not in the fire."

The storm is o'er—and hark ! a still small voice
Steals on the ear, to say, Jehovah's choice
   Is ever with the soft, meek, tender soul :
By soft, meek, tender ways He loves to draw
The sinner, startled by his ways of awe :
   Here is our Lord, and not where thunders roll.

Back then, complainer ; loath thy life no more,
Nor deem thyself upon a desert shore,
   Because the rocks the nearer prospect close.
Yet in fallen Israel are there hearts and eyes

That day by day in prayer like thine arise :
    Thou know'st them not, but their Creator knows.

Go, to the world return, nor fear to cast
Thy bread upon the waters, sure at last [h]
    In joy to find it after many days.
The work be thine, the fruit thy children's part :
Choose to believe, not see : sight tempts the heart
    From sober walking in true Gospel ways.

[h] Ecclesiastes xi. 1.

Tenth Sunday after Trinity.

And when he was come near, he beheld the city, and wept over it. St. Luke xix. 41.

WHY doth my Saviour weep
    At sight of Sion's bowers?
Shews it not fair from yonder steep,
    Her gorgeous crown of towers?
Mark well his holy pains:
    'Tis not in pride or scorn,
That Israel's King with sorrow stains
    His own triumphal morn.

It is not that his soul
    Is wandering sadly on,
In thought how soon at death's dark goal
    Their course will all be run,
Who now are shouting round
    Hosanna to their chief;
No thought like this in Him is found,
    This were a Conqueror's grief[1].

Or doth he feel the Cross
    Already in his heart,
The pain, the shame, the scorn, the loss?
    Feel even his God depart?
No : though he knew full well
    The grief that then shall be—
The grief that angels cannot tell—
    Our God in agony.

[1] Compare Herod. vii. 46.

It is not thus he mourns;
　　Such might be Martyr's tears,
When his last lingering look he turns
　　On human hopes and fears;
But hero ne'er or saint
　　The secret load might know,
With which His spirit waxeth faint;
　　His is a Saviour's woe.

" If thou hadst known, even thou,
　　" At least in this thy day,
" The message of thy peace ! but now
　　" 'Tis pass'd for aye away :
" Now foes shall trench thee round,
　　" And lay thee even with earth,
" And dash thy children to the ground,
　　" Thy glory and thy mirth."

And doth the Saviour weep
　　Over his people's sin,
Because we will not let him keep
　　The souls He died to win?
Ye hearts, that love the Lord,
　　If at this sight ye burn,
See that in thought, in deed, in word,
　　Ye hate what made Him mourn.

Eleventh Sunday after Trinity.

Is it a time to receive money, and to receive garments, and oliveyards, and vineyards, and sheep, and oxen, and menservants, and maidservants? 2 Kings v. 26.

I S this a time to plant and build,
　　Add house to house, and field to field,
When round our walls the battle lowers,
When mines are hid beneath our towers,
And watchful foes are stealing round
To search and spoil the holy ground?

Is this a time for moonlight dreams
Of love and home by mazy streams,
For Fancy with her shadowy toys,
Aerial hopes and pensive joys,
While souls are wandering far and wide
And curses swarm on every side?

No—rather steel thy melting heart
To act the martyr's sternest part,
To watch, with firm unshrinking eye,
Thy darling visions as they die,
Till all bright hopes, and hues of day
Have faded into twilight gray.

Yes—let them pass without a sigh,
And if the world seem dull and dry,
If long and sad thy lonely hours,
And winds have rent thy sheltering bowers,
Bethink thee what thou art and where,
A sinner in a life of care.

The fire of Heaven is soon to fall,
Thou know'st it, on this earthly ball ;
Then many a soul,·the price of blood,
Mark'd by th' Almighty's hand for good,
Shall feel the o'erflowing whirlwinds sweep—
And will the blessed Angels weep?

Then in his wrath shall God uproot
The trees He set, for lack of fruit,
And drown in rude tempestuous blaze
The towers His hand had deign'd to raise ;
In silence, ere that storm begin,
Count o'er His mercies and thy sin.

Pray only that thine aching heart,
From visions vain content to part,
Strong for Love's sake its woe to hide
May cheerful wait the cross beside,
Too happy if, that dreadful day,
Thy life be given thee for a prey ʲ.

Snatch'd sudden from th' avenging rod,
Safe in the bosom of thy God,
How wilt thou then look back, and smile
On thoughts that bitterest seem'd erewhile,
And bless the pangs that made thee see,
This was no world of rest for thee.

ʲ The Lord saith thus ; Behold, that which I have built will I
break down, and that which I have planted I will pluck up, even
this whole land. And seekest thou great things for thyself? seek
them not : for, behold, I will bring evil upon all flesh, saith the Lord :
but thy life will I give unto thee for a prey in all places whither
thou goest. *Jeremiah* xlv. 4, 5.

12

And looking up to heaven, he sighed, and saith unto him, Ephphatha, that is, Be opened. St. Mark vii. 34.

THE Son of God in doing good
   Was fain to look to heaven and sigh :
And shall the heirs of sinful blood
   Seek joy unmix'd in charity ?
God will not let Love's work impart
Full solace, lest it steal the heart ;
Be thou content in tears to sow,
Blessing, like Jesus, in thy woe.

He look'd to heaven, and sadly sigh'd—
   What saw my gracious Saviour there,
With fear and anguish to divide
   The joy of Heaven-accepted prayer ?
So o'er the bed where Lazarus slept
He to his Father groan'd and wept :
What saw he mournful in that grave,
Knowing himself so strong to save ?

O'erwhelming thoughts of pain and grief
   Over his sinking spirit sweep ;—
" What boots it gathering one lost leaf
   " Out of yon sere and wither'd heap,
" Where souls and bodies, hopes and joys,
" All that earth owns or sin destroys,
" Under the spurning hoof are cast,
" Or tossing in th' autumnal blast ?"

The deaf may hear the Saviour's voice,
   The fetter'd tongue its chain may break ;

But the deaf heart, the dumb by choice,
  The laggard soul, that will not wake,
The guilt that scorns to be forgiven ;—
These baffle e'en the spells of heaven ;
In thought of these, his brows benign,
Not even in healing cloudless shine.

No eye but His might ever bear
  To gaze all down that drear abyss,
Because none ever saw so clear
  The shore beyond of endless bliss :
The giddy waves so restless hurl'd,
The vex'd pulse of this feverish world,
He views and counts with steady sight,
Used to behold the Infinite.

But that in such communion high
  He hath a fount of strength within,
Sure His meek heart would break and die,
  O'erburthen'd by his brethren's sin ;
Weak eyes on darkness dare not gaze,
It dazzles like the noon-day blaze ;
But He who sees God's face may brook
On the true face of Sin to look.

What then shall wretched sinners do,
  When in their last, their hopeless day,
Sin, as it is, shall meet their view,
  God turn his face for aye away ?
Lord, by thy sad and earnest eye,
When Thou didst look to heaven and sigh ;
Thy voice, that with a word could chase
The dumb, deaf spirit from his place ;

As thou hast touch'd our ears, and taught
  Our tongues to speak thy praises plain

Quell thou each thankless godless thought
   That would make fast our bonds again,
From worldly strife, from mirth unblest,
Drowning thy music in the breast,
From foul reproach, from thrilling fears,
Preserve, good Lord, thy servants' ears.

From idle words, that restless throng,
   And haunt our hearts when we would pray,
From pride's false chime, and jarring wrong,
   Seal thou my lips, and guard the way :
For Thou hast sworn, that every ear,
Willing or loth, thy trump shall hear,
And every tongue unchained be
To own no hope, no God, but Thee.

Thirteenth Sunday after Trinity.

And he turned him unto his disciples, and said privately, Blessed are the eyes which see the things that ye see: for I tell you, that many prophets and kings have desired to see those things which ye see, and have not seen them; and to hear those things which ye hear, and have not heard them. St. Luke x. 23, 24.

ON Sinai's top, in prayer and trance,
　　Full forty nights and forty days
The Prophet watch'd for one dear glance
　　Of Thee and of thy ways :

Fasting he watch'd and all alone,
　　Wrapt in a still, dark, solid cloud,
The curtain of the Holy One
　　Drawn round him like a shroud .

So, separate from the world, his breast
　　Might duly take and strongly keep
The print of Heaven, tŏ be express'd
　　Ere long on Sion's steep [k].

There one by one his spirit saw,
　　Of things divine the shadows bright,
The pageant of God's perfect law ;
　　Yet felt not full delight.

Through gold and gems, a dazzling maze,
　　From veil to veil the vision led,

[k] See that thou make all things according to the pattern shewed to thee in the mount. *Hebrews* viii. 5.

And ended, where unearthly rays
  From o'er the Ark were shed.

Yet not that gorgeous place, nor aught
  Of human or angelic frame,
Could half appease his craving thought ;
  The void was still the same.

" Show me thy glory, gracious Lord !
  "'Tis Thee," he cries, " not thine, I seek[1]."
Nay, start not at so bold a word
  From man, frail worm and weak :

The spark of his first deathless fire
  Yet buoys him up, and high above
The holiest creature, dares aspire
  To the Creator's love.

The eye in smiles may wander round,
  Caught by earth's shadows as they fleet ;
But for the soul no help is found,
  Save Him who made it, meet.

Spite of yourselves, ye witness this, [m]
  Who blindly self or sense adore ;
Else wherefore leaving your own bliss
  Still restless ask ye more ?

This witness bore the saints of old
  When highest rapt and favour'd most,
Still seeking precious things untold,
  Not in fruition lost.

Canaan was theirs, and in it all
  The proudest hope of kings dare claim ;
Sion was theirs ; and at their call
  Fire from Jehovah came.

---

[1] Exodus xxxiii. 18.   [m] Pensées de Pascal, part i. art. viii.

Yet monarchs walk'd as pilgrims still
    In their own land, earth's pride and grace ;
And seers would mourn on Sion's hill
    Their Lord's averted face.

Vainly they tried the deeps to sound
    Even of their own prophetic thought,
When of Christ crucified and crown'd
    His Spirit in them taught :

But He their aching gaze repress'd
    Which sought behind the veil to see,
For not without us fully bless'd [n]
    Or perfect might they be.

The rays of the Almighty's face
    No sinner's eye might then receive ;
Only the meekest man found grace
    To see his skirts and live.

But we as in a glass espy
    The glory of His countenance,
Not in a whirlwind hurrying by
    The too presumptuous glance,

But with mild radiance every hour,
    From our dear Saviour's face benign
Bent on us with transforming power,
    Till we, too, faintly shine.

Sprinkled with His atoning blood
    Safely before our God we stand,
As on the rock the Prophet stood,
    Beneath His shadowing hand.

[n] That they without us should not be made perfect. *Hebrews* xi. 40.   [o] Exodus xxxiii. 20—23.

Bless'd eyes, which see the things we see !
   And yet this tree of life hath prov'd
To many a soul a poison tree,
   Beheld, and not belov'd.

So like an angel's is our bliss,
   Oh! thought to comfort and appal,
It needs must bring, if us'd amiss,
   An angel's hopeless fall.

Fourteenth Sunday after Trinity.

And Jesus answering said, Were there not ten cleansed? but where are the nine? There are not found that returned to give glory to God, save this stranger. St. Luke xvii. 17, 18.

TEN cleans'd, and only one remain !
  Who would have thought our nature's stain
Was dyed so foul, so deep in grain ?
    Even He who reads the heart,—
Knows what He gave and what we lost,
Sin's forfeit, and redemption's cost,—
By a short pang of wonder cross'd
    Seems at the sight to start :

Yet 'twas not wonder, but His love
Our wavering spirits would reprove,
That heaven-ward seem so free to move
    When earth can yield no more :
Then from afar on God we cry ;
But should the mist of woe roll by,
Not showers across an April sky
    Drift, when the storm is o'er,

Faster than those false drops and few
Fleet from the heart, a worthless dew.
What sadder scene can angels view
    Than self-deceiving tears,
Pour'd idly over some dark page
Of earlier life, though pride or rage
The record of to-day engage,
    A woe for future years ?

Spirits, that round the sick man's bed
Watch'd, noting down each prayer he made,
Were your unerring roll display'd,
    His pride of health to abase ;
Or, when soft showers in season fall
Answering a famish'd nation's call,
Should unseen fingers on the wall
    Our vows forgotten trace ;

How should we gaze in trance of fear !
Yet shines the light as thrilling clear
From heaven upon that scroll severe,
    " Ten cleans'd and one remain !"
Nor surer would the blessing prove
Of humbled hearts, that own thy love,
Should choral welcome from above
    Visit our senses plain :

That by Thy placid voice and brow,
With healing first, with comfort now,
Turn'd upon him, who hastes to bow
    Before thee, heart and knee ;
" Oh ! thou, who only would'st be blest,
" On thee alone my blessing rest !
" Rise, go thy way in peace, possess'd
    " For evermore of me."

*Consider the lilies of the field, how they
grow.* St. Matthew vi. 28.

S WEET nurslings of the vernal skies,
    Bath'd in soft airs, and fed with dew,
What more than magic in you lies,
    To fill the heart's fond view?
In childhood's sports, companions gay,
In sorrow, on Life's downward way,
How soothing! in our last decay
    Memorials prompt and true.

Relics ye are of Eden's bowers,
    As pure, as fragrant, and as fair,
As when ye crown'd the sunshine hours
    Of happy wanderers there.
Fall'n all beside—the world of life,
How is it stain'd with fear and strife!
In Reason's world what storms are rife,
    What passions range and glare!

But cheerful and unchang'd the while
    Your first and perfect form ye shew,
The same that won Eve's matron smile
    In the world's opening glow.
The stars of Heaven a course are taught
Too high above our human thought;—
Ye may be found if ye are sought,
    And as we gaze, we know.

Ye dwell beside our paths and homes.
    Our paths of sin, our homes of sorrow

And guilty man, where'er he roams,
　　Your innocent mirth may borrow.
The birds of air before us fleet,
They cannot brook our shame to meet—
But we may taste your solace sweet
　　And come again to-morrow.

Ye fearless in your nests abide—
　　Nor may we scorn, too proudly wise,
Your silent lessons, undescried
　　By all but lowly eyes :
For ye could draw th' admiring gaze
Of Him who worlds and hearts surveys :
Your order wild, your fragrant maze,
　　He taught us how to prize.

Ye felt your Maker's smile that hour,
　　As when He paus'd and own'd you good ;
His blessing on earth's primal bower,
　　Ye felt it all renew'd.
What care ye now, if winter's storm
Swee ᷉ ruthless o'er each silken form ?
Christ's blessing at your heart is warm,
　　Ye fear no vexing mood.

Alas ! of thousand bosoms kind,
　　That daily court you and caress,
How few the happy secret find
　　Of your calm loveliness !
" Live for to-day ! to-morrow's light
" To-morrow's cares shall bring to sight.
" Go sleep like closing flowers at night,
　　" And Heaven thy morn will bless."

Sixteenth Sunday after Trinity.

*I desire that ye faint not at my tribu-
lations for you, which is your glory.*
Ephesians iii. 13.

WISH not, dear friends, my pain away—
  Wish me a wise and thankful heart,
With God, in all my griefs, to stay,
  Nor from His lov'd correction start.

The dearest offering He can crave
  His portion in our souls to prove,
What is it to the gift He gave,
  The only Son of His dear love?

But we, like vex'd unquiet sprights,
  Will still be hovering, o'er the tomb,
Where buried lie our vain delights,
  Nor sweetly take a sinner's doom.

In Life's long sickness evermore
  Our thoughts are tossing to and fro :
We change our posture.o'er and o'er,
  But cannot rest, nor cheat our woe.

Were it not better to lie still,
  Let Him strike home and bless the rod,
Never so safe as when our will
  Yields undiscern'd by all but God?

Thy precious things, whate'er they be
  That haunt and vex thee, heart and brain,
Look to the Cross, and thou shalt see
  How thou may'st turn them all to gain.

Lovest thou praise? the Cross is shame :
　　Or ease? the Cross is bitter grief :
More pangs than tongue or heart can frame
　　Were suffer'd there without relief.

We of that altar would partake,
　　But cannot quit the cost—no throne
Is ours, to leave for Thy dear sake—
　　We cannot do as Thou hast done.

We cannot part with Heaven for Thee—
　　Yet guide us in thy track of love :
Let·us gaze on where light should be,
　　Though not a beam the clouds remove.

So wanderers ever fond and true
　　Look homeward through the evening sky,
Without a streak of heaven's soft blue
　　To aid Affection's dreaming eye.

The wanderer seeks his native bower,
　　And we will look and long for Thee,
And thank thee for each trying hour,
　　Wishing, not struggling, to be free.

Every man of the house of Israel that setteth up his idols in his heart, and putteth the stumbling-block of his iniquity before his face, and cometh to the Prophet; I the Lord will answer him that cometh according to the multitude of his idols. Ezekiel xiv. 4.

STATELY thy walls, and holy are the prayers,
   Which day and night before thine altars rise ;
Not statelier, towering o'er her marble stairs,
   Flash'd Sion's gilded dome to summer skies,
Not holier, while around him angels bow'd,
From Aaron's censer steam'd the spicy cloud,

Before the mercy-seat.   O Mother dear,
   Wilt thou forgive thy son one boding sigh ?
Forgive, if round thy towers he walk in fear,
   And tell thy jewels o'er with jealous eye ?
Mindful of that sad vision, which in thought P
From Chebar's plains the captive prophet brought

To see lost Sion's shame.   'Twas morning prime,
   And like a Queen new seated on her throne,
God's crowned mountain, as in happier time,
   Seem'd to rejoice in sunshine all her own :
So bright, while all in shade around her lay,
Her northern pinnacles had caught th' emerging ray.

The dazzling lines of her majestic roof
   Cross'd with as free a span the vault of Heaven,

P Ezekiel viii. 3.

As when twelve tribes knelt silently aloof,
  Ere God his answer to their king had given q,
Ere yet upon the new-built altar fell
The glory of the Lord, the Lord of Israel.

All seems the same : but enter in and see
  What idol shapes are on the wall pourtray'd r :
And watch their shameless and unholy glee,
  Who worship there in Aaron's robes array'd :
Hear Judah's maids the dirge to Thammuz pour s,
And mark her chiefs yon orient sun adore t.

Yet turn thee, Son of man—for worse than these
  Thou must behold : thy loathing were but lost
On dead men's crimes, and Jews' idolatries—
  Come, learn to tell aright thine own sins' cost,—
And sure their sin as far from equals thine,
As earthly hopes abus'd are less than hopes divine.

What if within His world, His church, our Lord
  Have enter'd thee, as in some temple gate,
Where, looking round, each glance might thee afford
  Some glorious earnest of thine high estate,
And thou, false heart and frail, hast turn'd from all
To worship pleasure's shadow on the wall?

If, when the Lord of Glory was in sight,
  Thou turn thy back upon that fountain clear,
To bow before the " little drop of light,"
  Which dim-eyed men call praise and glory here ;
What dost thou, but adore the sun, and scorn
Him at whose only word both sun and stars were born?

q 1 Kings viii. 5.   s Ezekiel viii. 14.
r Ezekiel viii. 10.   t Ezekiel viii. 16.

If, while around thee gales from Eden breathe,
   Thou hide thine eyes, to make thy peevish moan
Over some broken reed of earth beneath,
   Some darling of blind fancy dead and gone,
As wisely might'st thou in Jehovah's fane
Offer thy love and tears to Thammuz slain.

Turn thee from these, or dare not to enquire
   Of Him whose name is Jealous, lest in wrath
He hear and answer thine unblest desire :
   Far better we should cross his lightning's path
Than be according to our idols heard,
And God should take us at our own vain word.

Thou who hast deign'd the Christian's heart to call
   Thy Church and Shrine ; whene'er our rebel will
Would in that chosen home of thine instal
   Belial or Mammon, grant us not the ill
We blindly ask ; in very love refuse
Whate'er thou know'st our weakness would abuse.

Or rather help us, Lord, to choose the good,
   To pray for nought, to seek to none, but Thee,
Nor by " our daily bread " mean common food,
   Nor say, " From this world's evil set us free ;"
Teach us to love, with Christ, our sole true bliss,
Else, though in Christ's own words, we surely pray amiss.

13

Eighteenth Sunday after Trinity.

I will bring you into the wilderness of the people, and there will I plead with you face to face. Like as I pleaded with your fathers in the wilderness of the land of Egypt, so will I plead with you, saith the Lord God. Ezekiel xx. 35, 36.

I T is so—ope thine eyes, and see—
　　What view'st thou all around?
A desert, where iniquity
　　And knowledge both abound.

In the waste howling wilderness
　　The Church is wandering still [u],
Because we would not onward press
　　When close to Sion's hill.

Back to the world we faithless turn'd,
　　And far along the wild,
With labour lost and sorrow earn'd,
　　Our steps have been beguil'd.

Yet full before us, all the while,
　　The shadowing pillar stays,
The living waters brightly smile,
　　Th' eternal turrets blaze.

Yet Heaven is raining angels' bread
　　To be our daily food,
And fresh, as when it first was shed,
　　Springs forth the Saviour's blood.

[u] Revelations xii. 14.

From every region, race, and speech,
　　Believing myriads throng,
Till, far as sin and sorrow reach,
　　Thy grace is spread along;

Till sweetest nature, brightest art,
　　Their votive incense bring,
And every voice and every heart
　　Own Thee their God and King.

All own; but few, alas! will love;
　　Too like the recreant band
That with thy patient Spirit strove
　　Upon the Red-sea strand.

O Father of long-suffering grace,
　　Thou who hast sworn to stay
Pleading with sinners face to face
　　Through all their devious way.

How shall we speak to Thee, O Lord,
　　Or how in silence lie?
Look on us, and we are abhorr'd,
　　Turn from us, and we die.

Thy guardian fire, thy guiding cloud,
　　Still let them gild our wall,
Nor be our foes and thine allow'd
　　To see us faint and fall.

Too oft, within this camp of thine,
　　Rebellious murmurs rise;
Sin cannot bear to see thee shine
　　So awful to her eyes.

Fain would our lawless hearts escape,
　　And with the heathen be,

To worship every monstrous shape
    In fancied darkness free. ᵛ

Vain thought, that shall not be at all !
    Refuse we or obey,
Our ears have heard th' Almighty's call,
    We cannot be as they.

We cannot hope the heathen's doom,
    To whom God's Son is given,
Whose eyes have seen beyond the tomb,
    Who have the key of Heaven.

Weak tremblers on the edge of woe,
    Yet shrinking from true bliss,
Our rest must be "no rest below,"
    And let our prayer be this :

" Lord, wave again thy chastening rod,
    " Till every idol throne
" Crumble to dust, and Thou, O God,
    " Reign in our hearts alone.

" Bring all our wandering fancies home,
    " For Thou hast every spell,
" And 'mid the heathen where they roam,
    " Thou knowest, Lord, too well.

" Thou know'st our service sad and hard,
    " Thou know'st us fond and frail ;—
" Win us to be belov'd and spar'd
    " When all the world shall fail.

ᵛ That which cometh into your mind shall not be at all, that ye
say, We will be as the heathen, as the families of the countries, to
serve wood and stone. *Ezekiel* xx. 32.

" So when at last our weary days
  " Are well-nigh wasted here,
" And we can trace thy wondrous ways
  " In distance calm and clear,

" When in thy love and Israel's sin
  " We read our story true,
" We may not, all too late, begin
  " To wish our hopes were new :

" Long lov'd, long tried, long spar'd as they,
  " Unlike in this alone,
" That, by thy grace, our hearts shall stay
  " For evermore thine own."

Nineteenth Sunday after Trinity.

Then Nebuchadnezzar the king was astonied, and rose up in haste, and spake, and said unto his counsellors, Did not we cast three men bound into the midst of the fire? They answered and said unto the king, True, O king. He answered and said, Lo, I see four men loose, walking in the midst of the fire, and they have no hurt; and the form of the fourth is like the Son of God. Daniel iii. 24, 25.

WHEN Persecution's torrent blaze
    Wraps the unshrinking Martyr's head ;
When fade all earthly flowers and bays,
    When summer friends are gone and fled,
Is he alone in that dark hour,
Who owns the Lord of love and power ?

Or waves there not around his brow
    A wand no human arm may wield,
Fraught with a spell no angels know,
    His steps to guide, his soul to shield ?
Thou, Saviour, art his charmed bower,
His magic ring, his rock, his tower.

And when the wicked ones behold
    Thy favourites walking in thy light,
Just as, in fancied triumph bold,
    They deem'd them lost in deadly night,
Amaz'd they cry, " What spell is this,
" Which turns their sufferings all to bliss ?

" How are they free whom we had bound,
   " Upright, whom in the gulf we cast ?
" What wondrous helper have they found
   " To screen them from the scorching blast ?
" Three were they—who hath made them four ?
" And sure a form divine he wore,

" Even like the Son of God."   So cried
   The Tyrant, when in one fierce flame
The martyrs liv'd, the murderers died :
   Yet knew he not what angel came
To make the rushing fire-flood seem
Like summer breeze by woodland stream [x].

He knew not, but there are who know :
   The Matron, who alone hath stood,
When not a prop seem'd left below,
   The first lorn hour of widowhood,
Yet cheer'd and cheering all, the while,
With sad but unaffected smile ;—

The Father, who his vigil keeps
   By the sad couch whence hope hath flown,
Watching the eye where reason sleeps,
   Yet in his heart can mercy own,
Still sweetly yielding to the rod,
Still loving man, still thanking God ;—

The Christian Pastor, bow'd to earth
   With thankless toil, and vile esteem'd,
Still travailing in second birth
   Of souls that will not be redeem'd,
Yet stedfast set to do his part,
And fearing most his own vain heart ;—

[x] *Song of the Three Children*, ver. 27. As it had been a moist
whistling wind.

These know : on these look long and well,
  Cleansing thy sight by prayer and faith,
And thou shalt know what secret spell
  Preserves them in their living death :
Through sevenfold flames thine eye shall see
The Saviour walking with his faithful Three.

Twentieth Sunday after Trinity.

Hear ye, O mountains, the Lord's controversy, and ye strong foundations of the earth. Micah vi. 2.

WHERE is thy favour'd haunt, eternal Voice,
　　The region of thy choice,
Where, undisturb'd by sin and earth, the soul
　　Owns thine entire control ?—
'Tis on the mountain's summit dark and high,
　　When storms are hurrying by :
'Tis 'mid the strong foundations of the earth,
　　Where torrents have their birth.

No sounds of worldly toil ascending there,
　　Mar the full burst of prayer ;
Lone Nature feels that she may freely breathe,
　　And round us and beneath
Are heard her sacred tones : the fitful sweep
　　Of winds across the steep,
Through wither'd bents—romantic note and clear,
　　Meet for a hermit's ear,—

The wheeling kite's wild solitary cry,
　　And, scarcely heard so high,
The dashing waters when the air is still
　　From many a torrent rill
That winds unseen beneath the shaggy fell,
　　Track'd by the blue mist well :
Such sounds as make deep silence in the heart
　　For Thought to do her part.

'Tis then we hear the voice of God within,
　　Pleading with care and sin :

" Child of my love ! how have I wearied thee ?
    " Why wilt thou err from me ?
" Have I not brought thee from the house of slaves,
    " Parted the drowning waves,
" And set my saints before thee in the way,
    " Lest thou should'st faint or stray ?

" What ? was the promise made to thee alone ?
    " Art thou th' excepted one ?
" An heir of glory without grief or pain ?
    " O vision false and vain !
" There lies thy cross ; beneath it meekly bow ;
    " It fits thy stature now :
" Who scornful pass it with averted eye,
    " 'Twill crush them by and by.

" Raise thy repining eyes, and take true measure
    " Of thine eternal treasure ;
" The Father of thy Lord can grudge thee nought,
    " The world for thee was bought,
" And as this landscape broad—earth, sea, and sky,—
    " All centres in thine eye,
" So all God does, if rightly understood,
    " Shall work thy final good."

Twenty-first Sunday after Trinity.

The vision is yet for an appointed time, but at the end it shall speak; and not lie: though it tarry, wait for it; because it will surely come, it will not tarry. Habakkuk ii. 3.

THE morning mist is clear'd away,
　Yet still the face of heaven is grey,
Nor yet th' autumnal breeze has stirr'd the grove,
　Faded yet full, a paler green
　Skirts soberly the tranquil scene,
The red-breast warbles round this leafy cove.

　Sweet messenger of " calm decay,"
　Saluting sorrow as you may,
As one still bent to find or make the best,
　In thee, and in this quiet mead
　The lesson of sweet peace I read,
Rather in all to be resign'd than blest.

　'Tis a low chant, according well
　With the soft solitary knell,
As homeward from some grave belov'd we turn,
　Or by some holy death-bed dear,
　Most welcome to the chasten'd ear
Of her whom heaven is teaching how to mourn.

　O cheerful tender strain ! the heart
　That duly bears with you its part,
Singing so thankful to the dreary blast,
　Though gone and spent its joyous prime,
　And on the world's autumnal time,
Mid wither'd hues and sere, its lot be cast :

That is the heart for thoughtful seer,
　Watching, in trance nor dark nor clear ʸ,
Th' astounding Future as it nearer draws :
　　His spirit calm'd the storm to meet,
　　Feeling the rock beneath his feet,
And tracing through the cloud th' eternal Cause.

That is the heart for watchman true
　Waiting to see what God will do,
As o'er the Church the gathering twilight falls :
　　No more he strains his wistful eye,
　　If chance the golden hours be nigh,
By youthful Hope seen beaming round her walls.

Forc'd from his shadowy paradise,
　His thoughts to Heaven the steadier rise :
There seek his answer when the world reproves :
　　Contented in his darkling round
　　If only he be faithful found,
When from the east th' eternal morning moves.

Note :　The expression, "calm decay," is borrowed from a friend : by whose kind permission the following stanzas are here inserted.

TO THE RED-BREAST.

Unheard in summer's flaring ray,
　Pour forth thy notes, sweet singer,
Wooing the stillness of the autumn day :
　　Bid it a moment linger,
　　　Nor fly
Too soon from winter's scowling eye.

The blackbird's song at even-tide,
　And hers, who gay ascends,
Filling the heavens far and wide,
　　Are sweet.　But none so blends,
　　　As thine,
With calm decay, and peace divine.

ʸ It shall come to pass in that day, that the night shall not be clear nor dark. *Zechariah* xiv. 6.

Lord, how oft shall my brother sin against me, and I forgive him?
St. Matthew xviii. 21.

W HAT liberty so glad and gay,
    As where the mountain boy,
Reckless of regions far away,
    A prisoner lives in joy?

The dreary sounds of crowded earth,
    The cries of camp or town,
Never untun'd his lonely mirth,
    Nor drew his visions down.

The snow-clad peaks of rosy light
    That meet his morning view,
The thwarting cliffs that bound his sight,
    They bound his fancy too.

Two ways alone his roving eye
    For aye may onward go,
Or in the azure deep on high,
    Or darksome mere below.

O blest restraint! more blessed range!
    Too soon the happy child
His nook of homely thought will change
    For life's seducing wild:

Too soon his alter'd day dreams show
    This earth a boundless space,
With sun-bright pleasures to and fro
    Sporting in joyous race:

While of his narrowing heart each year,
 Heaven less and less will fill,
Less keenly, through his grosser ear,
 The tones of mercy thrill.

It must be so : else wherefore falls
 The Saviour's voice unheard,
While from His pardoning Cross He calls,
 " O spare as I have spar'd "?

By our own niggard rule we try
 The hope to suppliants given ;
We mete out love, as if our eye
 Saw to the end of heaven.

Yes, ransom'd sinner ! wouldst thou know
 How often to forgive,
How dearly to embrace thy foe,
 Look where thou hop'st to live :

When thou hast told those isles of light,
 And fancied all beyond,
Whatever owns, in depth or height,
 Creation's wondrous bond ;

Then in their solemn pageant learn
 Sweet mercy's praise to see :
Their Lord resign'd them all, to earn
 The bliss of pardoning thee.

*Who shall change our vile body, that
it may be fashioned like unto his
glorious body, according to the
working whereby he is able even
to subdue all things unto himself.*
Philippians iii. 21.

R ED o'er the forest peers the setting sun,
   The line of yellow light dies fast away
That crown'd the eastern copse : and chill and dun
   Falls on the moor the brief November day.

Now the tir'd hunter winds a parting note,
   And Echo bids good-night from every glade ;
Yet wait awhile, and see the calm leaves float
   Each to his rest beneath their parent shade.

How like decaying life they seem to glide !
   And yet no second spring have they in store,
But where they fall forgotten to abide,
   Is all their portion, and they ask no more.

Soon o'er their heads blithe April airs shall sing,
   A thousand wild-flowers round them shall unfold,
The green buds glisten in the dews of Spring,
   And all be vernal rapture as of old.

Unconscious they in waste oblivion lie,
   In all the world of busy life around
No thought of them ; in all the bounteous sky
   No drop, for them, of kindly influence found.

Man's portion is to die and rise again—
   Yet he complains, while these unmurmuring part

With their sweet lives, as pure from sin and stain,
    As his when Eden held his virgin heart.

And haply half unblam'd his murmuring voice
    Might sound in heaven, were all his second life
Only the first renew'd—the heathen's choice,
    A round of listless joy and weary strife.

For dreary were this earth, if earth were all,
    Though brighten'd oft by dear Affection's kiss ;—
Who for the spangles wears the funeral pall ?
    But catch a gleam beyond it, and 'tis bliss.

Heavy and dull this frame of limbs and heart,
    Whether slow creeping on cold earth, or borne
On lofty steed, or loftier prow, we dart
    O'er wave or field : yet breezes laugh to scorn

Our puny speed, and birds, and clouds in heaven,
    And fish, like living shafts that pierce the main,
And stars that shoot through freezing air at even—
    Who but would follow, might he break his chain ?

And thou shalt break it soon ; the grovelling worm
    Shall find his wings, and soar as fast and free
As his transfigur'd Lord with lightning form
    And snowy vest—such grace He won for thee,

When from the grave He sprung at dawn of morn,
    And led through boundless air thy conquering road,
Leaving a glorious track, where saints new-born
    Might fearless follow to their blest abode.

But first, by many a stern and fiery blast
    The world's rude furnace must thy blood refine,

And many a gale of keenest woe be pass'd,
   Till every pulse beat true to airs divine,

Till every limb obey the mounting soul,
   The mounting soul, the call by Jesus given.
He who the stormy heart can so control
   The laggard body soon will waft to heaven.

Twenty-fourth Sunday after Trinity.

The heart knoweth his own bitterness; and a stranger doth not intermeddle with his joy. Proverbs xiv. 10.

WHY should we faint and fear to live alone,
   Since all alone, so Heaven has will'd, we die[z],
Nor even the tenderest heart, and next our own,
   Knows half the reasons why we smile and sigh?

Each in his hidden sphere of joy or woe
   Our hermit spirits dwell, and range apart,
Our eyes see all around in gloom or glow—
   Hues of their own, fresh borrow'd from the heart.

And well it is for us our God should feel
   Alone our secret throbbings : so our prayer
May readier spring to Heaven, nor spend its zeal
   On cloud-born idols of this lower air.

For if one heart in perfect sympathy
   Beat with another, answering love for love,
Weak mortals, all entranc'd, on earth would lie,
   Nor listen for those purer strains above.

Or what if Heaven for once its searching light
   Lent to some partial eye, disclosing all
The rude bad thoughts, that in our bosom's night
   Wander at large, nor heed Love's gentle thrall?

Who would not shun the dreary uncouth place?
   As if, fond leaning where her infant slept,

        [z] Je mourrai seul. *Pascal.*

A mother's arm a serpent should embrace :
  So might we friendless live, and die unwept.

Then keep the softening veil in mercy drawn,
  Thou who canst love us, tho' Thou read us true ;
As on the bosom of th' aerial lawn
  Melts in dim haze each coarse ungentle hue.

So too may soothing Hope thy leave enjoy
  Sweet visions of long sever'd hearts to frame :
Though absence may impair, or cares annoy,
  Some constant mind may draw us still the same.

We in dark dreams are tossing to and fro,
  Pine with regret, or sicken with despair,
The while she bathes us in her own chaste glow,
  And with our memory wings her own fond prayer.

O bliss of child-like innocence, and love
  Tried to old age ! creative power to win,
And raise new worlds, where happy fancies rove,
  Forgetting quite this grosser world of sin.

Bright are their dreams, because their thoughts are clear,
  Their memory cheering : but th' earth-stained spright,
Whose wakeful musings are of guilt and fear,
  Must hover nearer earth, and less in light.

Farewell, for her, th' ideal scenes so fair—
  Yet not farewell her hope, since Thou hast deign'd,
Creator of all hearts ! to own and share
  The woe of what Thou mad'st, and we have stain'd.

Thou know'st our bitterness—our joys are thine [a]—
  No stranger Thou to all our wanderings wild :

* [a] Thou hast known my soul in adversities. *Psalm* xxxi. 7.

Nor could we bear to think, how every line
    Of us, thy darken'd likeness and defil'd,

Stands in full sunshine of thy piercing eye,
    But that thou call'st us Brethren : sweet repose
Is in that word—the Lord who dwells on high
    Knows all, yet loves us better than He knows.

*The hoary head is a crown of glory,
if it be found in the way of
righteousness.* Proverbs xvi. 31.

THE bright hair'd morn is glowing
   O'er emerald meadows gay,
With many a clear gem strowing
   The early shepherd's way.
Ye gentle elves, by Fancy seen
   Stealing away with night
To slumber in your leafy screen,
   Tread more than airy light.

And see what joyous greeting
   The sun through heaven has shed,
Though fast yon shower be fleeting,
   His beams have faster sped.
For lo ! above the western haze
   High towers the rainbow arch
In solid span of purest rays :
   How stately is its march !

Pride of the dewy morning !
   The swain's experienc'd eye
From thee takes timely warning,
   Nor trusts the gorgeous sky.
For well he knows, such dawnings gay
   Bring noons of storm and shower,
And travellers linger on the way
   Beside the sheltering bower.

Even so, in hope and trembling
   Should watchful shepherd view

His little lambs assembling,
    With glance both kind and true ;
'Tis not the eye of keenest blaze,
    Nor the quick-swelling breast,
That soonest thrills at touch of praise—
    These do not please him best.

But voices low and gentle,
    And timid glances shy,
That seem for aid parental
    To sue all wistfully,
Still pressing, longing to be right,
    Yet fearing to be wrong—
In these the Pastor dares delight,
    A lamb-like, Christ-like throng.

These in Life's distant even
    Shall shine serenely bright,
As in th' autumnal heaven
    Mild rainbow tints at night,
When the last shower is stealing down,
    And ere they sink to rest,
The sun-beams weave a parting crown
    For some sweet woodland nest.

The promise of the morrow
    Is glorious on that eve,
Dear as the holy sorrow
    When good men cease to live.
When brightening ere it die away
    Mounts up their altar flame,
Still tending with intenser ray
    To Heaven whence first it came.

Say not it dies, that glory,
    'Tis caught unquench'd on high,

Those saint-like brows so hoary
  Shall wear it in the sky.
No smile is like the smile of death,
  When all good musings past
Rise wafted with the parting breath,
  The sweetest thought the last.

WILL God indeed with fragments bear,
　　Snatch'd late from the decaying year?
Or can the Saviour's blood endear
　　The dregs of a polluted life?
When down th' o'erwhelming current tost,
Just ere he sink for ever lost,
The sailor's untried arms are cross'd
In agonizing prayer, will Ocean cease her strife?

　Sighs that exhaust but not relieve,
　Heart-rending sighs, O spare to heave
　A bosom freshly taught to grieve
　　　For lavish'd hours and love misspent!
　Now through her round of holy thought
　The Church our annual steps has brought,
　But we no holy fire have caught—
Back on the gaudy world our wilful eyes were bent.

　Too soon th' ennobling carols, pour'd
　To hymn the birth-night of the Lord,
　Which duteous Memory should have stor'd
　　　For thankful echoing all the year—
　Too soon those airs have pass'd away;
　Nor long within the heart would stay
　The silence of Christ's dying day,
Profan'd by worldly mirth, or scar'd by worldly fear.

　Some strain of hope and victory
　On Easter wings might lift us high;

A little while we sought the sky :
    And when the Spirit's beacon fires
On every hill began to blaze,
Lightening the world with glad amaze,
Who but must kindle while they gaze?
But faster than she soars, our earth-bound Fancy tires.

Nor yet for these, nor all the rites,
By which our Mother's voice invites
Our God to bless our home delights,
    And sweeten every secret tear :—
The funeral dirge, the marriage vow,
The hallow'd font where parents bow,
And now elate and trembling now
To the Redeemer's feet their new-found treasures
        bear :—

Not for the Pastor's gracious arm
Stretch'd out to bless—a Christian charm
To dull the shafts of worldly harm :—
    Nor, sweetest, holiest, best of all,
For the dear feast of Jesus dying,
Upon that altar ever lying,
Where souls with sacred hunger sighing
Are call'd to sit and eat, while angels prostrate fall :—

No, not for each and all of these,
Have our frail spirits found their ease.
The gale that stirs th' autumnal trees
    Seems tun'd as truly to our hearts
As when, twelve weary months ago,
'Twas moaning bleak, so high and low,
You would have thought Remorse and Woe
Had taught the innocent air their sadly thrilling parts.

Is it, Christ's light is too divine,
We dare not hope like Him to shine ?

But see, around His dazzling shrine
    Earth's gems the fire of heaven have caught ;
Martyrs and saints—each glorious day
Dawning in order on our way—
Remind us, how our darksome clay
May keep th' ethereal warmth our new Creator brought.

These we have scorn'd, O false and frail !
And now once more th' appalling tale,
How love divine may woo and fail,
    Of our lost year in heaven is told—
What if as far our life were past,
Our weeks all number'd to the last,
With time and hope behind us cast,
And all our work to do with palsied hands and cold ?

O watch and pray ere Advent dawn !
For thinner than the subtlest lawn
'Twixt thee and death the veil is drawn.
    But Love too late can never glow :
The scatter'd fragments Love can glean,
Refine the dregs, and yield us clean
To regions where one thought serene
Breathes sweeter than whole years of sacrifice below.

St. Andrew's Day.

He first findeth his own brother Simon, and saith unto him, We have found the Messias . . . And he brought him to Jesus. St. John i. 41, 42.

WHEN brothers part for manhood's race,
　What gift may most endearing prove
To keep fond memory in her place,
　And certify a brother's love?

'Tis true, bright hours together told,
　And blissful dreams in secret shar'd,
Serene or solemn, gay or bold,
　Shall last in fancy unimpair'd.

Even round the death-bed of the good
　Such dear remembrances will hover,
And haunt us with no vexing mood
　When all the cares of earth are over.

But yet our craving spirits feel,
　We shall live on, though Fancy die,
And seek a surer pledge—a seal
　Of love to last eternally.

Who art thou, that would'st grave thy name
　Thus deeply in a brother's heart?
Look on this saint, and learn to frame
　Thy love-charm with true Christian art.

First seek thy Saviour out, and dwell
　Beneath the shadow of his roof,

Till thou have scann'd his features well,
   And known Him for the Christ by proof;

Such proof as they are sure to find,
   Who spend with him their happy days,
Clean hands, and a self-ruling mind
   Ever in tune for love and praise.

Then, potent with the spell of heaven,
   Go, and thine erring brother gain,
Entice him home to be forgiven,
   Till he, too, see his Saviour plain.

Or, if before thee in the race,
   Urge him with thine advancing tread,
Till, like twin stars, with even pace,
   Each lucid course be duly sped.

No fading frail memorial give
   To soothe his soul when thou art gone,
But wreaths of hope for aye to live,
   And thoughts of good together done.

That so, before the judgment-seat,
   Though chang'd and glorified each face,
Not unremember'd ye may meet
   For endless ages to embrace.

St. Thomas' Day.

Thomas, because thou hast seen me, thou hast believed: blessed are they that have not seen, and yet have believed.
St. John xx. 29.

WE were not by when Jesus came [b],
    But round us, far and near,
We see his trophies, and his name
    In choral echoes hear.
In a fair ground our lot is cast,
As in the solemn week that past,
While some might doubt, but all ador'd [c],
Ere the whole widow'd Church had seen her risen Lord.

Slowly, as then, His bounteous hand
    The golden chain unwinds,
Drawing to Heaven with gentlest band
    Wise hearts and loving minds.
Love sought him first—at dawn of morn [d]
From her sad couch she sprang forlorn,
She sought to weep with Thee alone,
And saw thine open grave, and knew that Thou wert
        gone.

Reason and Faith at once set out [e]
    To search the Saviour's tomb ;
Faith faster runs, but waits without,
    As fearing to presume

[b] Thomas, one of the twelve, called Didymus, was not with them when Jesus came. *St. John* xx. 24.

[c] When they saw him, they worshipped him : but some doubted. *St. Matthew* xxviii. 17.

[d] St. Mary Magdalene's visit to the sepulchre.

[e] St. Peter and St. John.

Till Reason enter in, and trace
Christ's relics round the holy place—
" Here lay His limbs, and here His sacred head,
" And who was by, to make his new-forsaken bed ?"

Both wonder, one believes—but while
    They muse on all at home,
No thought can tender Love beguile
    From Jesus' grave to roam.
Weeping she stays till He appear—
Her witness first the Church must hear—
All joy to souls that can rejoice
With her at earliest call of His dear gracious voice.

Joy too to those, who love to talk
    In secret how He died,
Though with seal'd eyes awhile they walk,
    Nor see Him at their side ;
Most like the faithful pair are they,
Who once to Emmaus took their way,
Half darkling, till their Master shed
His glory on their souls, made known in breaking bread.

Thus, ever brighter and more bright,
    On those he came to save
The Lord of new-created light
    Dawn'd gradual from the grave :
Till pass'd th' enquiring daylight hour,
And with clos'd door in silent bower
The Church in anxious musing sate,
As one who for redemption still had long to wait.

Then, gliding through th' unopening door,
    Smooth without step or sound,
" Peace to your souls," He said—no more—
    They own him, kneeling round.

Eye, ear, and hand, and loving heart,
Body and soul in every part,
Successive made His witnesses that hour,
Cease not in all the world to shew his saving power.

Is there, on earth, a spirit frail,
    Who fears to take their word,
Scarce daring, through the twilight pale,
    To think he sees the Lord ?
With eyes too tremblingly awake
To bear with dimness for His sake ?
Read and confess the hand divine
That drew thy likeness here so true in every line.

For all thy rankling doubts so sore,
    Love thou thy Saviour still,
Him for thy Lord and God adore,
    And ever do His will.
Though vexing thoughts may seem to last,
Let not thy soul be quite o'ercast ;—
Soon will He shew thee all His wounds, and say
" Long have I known thy name f—know thou my face
        " alway."

f In Exodus xxxiii. 17, God says to Moses, "I know thee by name ;" meaning, "I bear especial favour towards thee." Thus our Saviour speaks to St. Thomas by name in the place here referred to.

The Conversion of St. Paul.

And he fell to the earth, and heard a voice saying unto him, Saul, Saul, why persecutest thou me? And he said, Who art Thou, Lord? And the Lord said, I am Jesus whom thou persecutest. Acts ix. 4, 5.

THE midday sun, with fiercest glare,
  Broods o'er the hazy, twinkling air ;
    Along the level sand
The palm-tree's shade unwavering lies,
Just as thy towers, Damascus, rise
    To greet yon wearied band.

The leader of that martial crew
Seems bent some mighty deed to do,
    So steadily he speeds,
With lips firm clos'd and fixed eye,
Like warrior when the fight is nigh,
    Nor talk nor landscape heeds.

What sudden blaze is round him pour'd,
As though all heaven's refulgent hoard
    In one rich glory shone ?
One moment—and to earth he falls :
What voice his inmost heart appals ?—
    Voice heard by him alone.

For to the rest both words and form
Seem lost in lightning and in storm,
    While Saul, in wakeful trance,
Sees deep within that dazzling field
His persecuted Lord reveal'd
    With keen yet pitying glance :

And hears the meek upbraiding call
As gently on his spirit fall
    As if th' Almighty Son
Were prisoner yet in this dark earth,
Nor had proclaim'd his royal birth,
    Nor his great power begun.

" Ah wherefore persecut'st thou me ? "
He heard and saw, and sought to free
    His strain'd eye from the sight :
But Heaven's high magic bound it there,
Still gazing, though untaught to bear
    Th' insufferable light.

" Who art thou, Lord ?" he falters forth :—
So shall Sin ask of heaven and earth
    At the last awful day.
" When did we see thee suffering nigh [g],
" And pass'd thee with unheeding eye ?
    " Great God of judgment, say ! "

Ah ! little dream our listless eyes
What glorious presence they despise,
    While, in our noon of life,
To power or fame we rudely press.—
Christ is at hand, to scorn or bless,
    Christ suffers in our strife.

And though heaven gate long since have clos'd,
And our dear Lord in bliss repos'd
    High above mortal ken,
To every ear in every land,
Though meek ears only understand,
    He speaks as He did then.

[g] St. Matthew xxv. 44.

15

" Ah wherefore persecute ye me ?
" 'Tis hard, ye so in love should be
    " With your own endless woe.
" Know, though at God's right hand I live,
" I feel each wound ye reckless give
    " To the least saint below.

" I in your care my brethren left,
" Not willing ye should be bereft
    " Of waiting on your Lord.
" The meanest offering ye can make—
" A drop of water—for love's sake [h],
    " In Heaven, be sure, is stor'd."

O by those gentle tones and dear,
When Thou hast stay'd our wild career,
    Thou only hope of souls,
Ne'er let us cast one look behind,
But in the thought of Jesus find
    What every thought controuls.

As to thy last Apostle's heart
Thy lightning glance did then impart
    Zeal's never-dying fire,
So teach us on thy shrine to lay
Our hearts, and let them day by day
    Intenser blaze and higher.

And as each mild and winning note—
Like pulses that round harp-strings float,
    When the full strain is o'er—
Left lingering on his inward ear
Music, that taught, as death drew near,
    Love's lesson more and more :

[h] St. Matthew x. 42.

So, as we walk our earthly round,
Still may the echo of that sound
    Be in our memory stor'd :
" Christians ! behold your happy state :
" Christ is in these, who round you wait ;
    " Make much of your dear Lord ! "

The Purification.

Blessed are the pure in heart: for they shall see God. St. Matthew v. 8.

BLESS'D are the pure in heart,
　　For they shall see our God,
The secret of the Lord is theirs,
　　Their soul is Christ's abode.

Might mortal thought presume
　　To guess an angel's lay,
Such are the notes that echo through
　　The courts of Heaven to-day.

Such the triumphal hymns
　　On Sion's Prince that wait,
In high procession passing on
　　Towards His temple-gate.

Give ear, ye kings—bow down,
　　Ye rulers of the earth—
This, this is He ; your Priest by grace,
　　Your God and King by birth.

No pomp of earthly guards
　　Attends with sword and spear,
And all-defying, dauntless look,
　　Their monarch's way to clear :

Yet are there more with him
　　Than all that are with you—
The armies of the highest Heaven,
　　All righteous, good, and true.

Spotless their robes and pure,
Dipp'd in the sea of light,
That hides the unapproached shrine
From men's and angels' sight.

His throne, thy bosom blest,
O Mother undefil'd—
That throne, if aught beneath the skies,
Beseems the sinless child.

Lost in high thoughts, " whose son
" The wondrous Babe might prove,
Her guileless husband walks beside,
Bearing the hallow'd dove ;

Meet emblem of His vow,
Who, on this happy day,
His dove-like soul—best sacrifice—
Did on God's altar lay.

But who is he, by years
Bow'd, but erect in heart,
Whose prayers are struggling with his tears ?
" Lord, let me now depart.

" Now hath thy servant seen
" Thy saving health, O Lord :
" 'Tis time that I depart in peace,
" According to thy word."

Yet swells the pomp : one more
Comes forth to bless her God :
Full fourscore years, meek widow, she
Her heaven-ward way hath trod.

She who to earthly joys
So long had given farewell,

Now sees, unlook'd for, Heaven on earth,
    Christ in His Israel.

    Wide open from that hour
    The temple-gates are set,
And still the saints rejoicing there
    The holy Child have met.

    Now count his train to-day,
    And who may meet him, learn :
Him child-like sires, meek maidens find,
    Where pride can nought discern.

    Still to the lowly soul
    He doth himself impart,
And for His cradle and His throne
    Chooseth the pure in heart.

St. Matthias' Day.

Wherefore of these men which have companied with us all the time that the Lord Jesus went in and out among us, beginning from the baptism of John, unto that same day that he was taken up from us, must one be ordained to be a witness with us of his resurrection. Acts i. 21, 22.

WHO is God's chosen priest?
    He, who on Christ stands waiting day
        and night,
Who trac'd His holy steps, nor ever ceas'd,
    From Jordan banks to Bethphage height :

    Who hath learn'd lowliness
From his Lord's cradle, patience from His cross ;
Whom poor men's eyes and hearts consent to bless ;
    To whom, for Christ, the world is loss ;

    Who both in agony
Hath seen Him and in glory ; and in both
Own'd Him divine, and yielded, nothing loth,
    Body and soul, to live and die,

    In witness of his Lord,
In humble following of his Saviour dear :
This is the man to wield th' unearthly sword,
    Warring unharm'd with sin and fear.

    But who can e'er suffice—
What mortal—for this more than angels' task,
Winning or losing souls, Thy life-blood's price?
    The gift were too divine to ask,

But Thou hast made it sure
By Thy dear promise to Thy Church and Bride,
That Thou, on earth, would'st aye with her endure,
    Till earth to Heaven be purified.

Thou art her only spouse,
Whose arm supports her, on whose faithful breast
Her persecuted head she meekly bows,
    Sure pledge of her eternal rest.

Thou, her unerring guide,
Stayest her fainting steps along the wild ;
Thy mark is on the bowers of lust and pride,
    That she may pass them undefil'd.

Who then, uncall'd by Thee,
Dare touch thy spouse, thy very self below ?
Or who dare count him summon'd worthily,
    Except thine hand and seal he show ?

Where can thy seal be found,
But on the chosen seed, from age to age
By thine anointed heralds duly crown'd,
    As kings and priests thy war to wage ?

Then fearless walk we forth,
Yet full of trembling, Messengers of God :
Our warrant sure, but doubting of our worth,
    By our own shame alike and glory aw'd.

Dread Searcher of the hearts,
Thou who didst seal by thy descending Dove
Thy servant's choice, O help us in our parts,
    Else helpless found, to learn and teach thy love.

The Annunciation of the Blessed Virgin Mary.

And the angel came in unto her, and said, Hail, thou that art highly favoured, the Lord is with thee : blessed art thou among women.
St. Luke i. 28.

OH Thou who deign'st to sympathize
　　With all our frail and fleshly ties,
　　　　Maker yet Brother dear,
Forgive the too presumptuous thought,
If, calming wayward grief, I sought
　　　　To gaze on Thee too near.

Yet sure 'twas not presumption, Lord,
'Twas thine own comfortable word
　　　　That made the lesson known :
Of all the dearest bonds we prove,
Thou countest sons' and mothers' love
　　　　Most sacred, most thine own.

When wandering here a little span,
Thou took'st on Thee to rescue man,
　　　　Thou hadst no earthly sire :
That wedded love we prize so dear,
As if our heaven and home were here,
　　　　It lit in Thee no fire.

On no sweet sister's faithful breast
Wouldst thou thine aching forehead rest,
　　　　On no kind brother lean :
But who, O perfect filial heart,
E'er did like Thee a true son's part,
　　　　Endearing, firm, serene ?

Thou wept'st, meek maiden, mother mild,
Thou wept'st upon thy sinless child,
　　Thy very heart was riven :
And yet, what mourning matron here
Would deem thy sorrows bought too dear
　　By all on this side Heaven ?

A son that never did amiss,
That never sham'd his mother's kiss,
　　Nor cross'd her fondest prayer :
Even from the tree he deign'd to bow
For her his agonized brow,
　　Her, his sole earthly care.

Ave Maria ! blessed Maid !
Lily of Eden's fragrant shade,
　　Who can express the love
That nurtur'd thee so pure and sweet,
Making thy heart a shelter meet
　　For Jesus' holy Dove ?

Ave Maria ! Mother blest,
To whom caressing and caress'd,
　　Clings the Eternal Child ;
Favour'd beyond Archangels' dream,
When first on thee with tenderest gleam
　　Thy new-born Saviour smil'd :—

Ave Maria ! Thou whose name
All but adoring love may claim,
　　Yet may we reach thy shrine ;
For He, thy Son and Saviour, vows
To crown all lowly lofty brows
　　With love and joy like thine.

Bless'd is the womb that bare Him—bless'd [i]
The bosom where his lips were press'd,
    But rather bless'd are they
Who hear his word and keep it well,
The living homes where Christ shall dwell,
    And never pass away.

[i] St. Luke xi. 27, 28.

St. Mark's Day.

And the contention was so sharp between them, that they departed asunder one from the other. Acts xv. 39.

Compare 2 Tim. iv. 11. *Take Mark, and bring him with thee : for he is profitable to me for the ministry.*

O H ! who shall dare in this frail scene
On holiest happiest thoughts to lean,
On Friendship, Kindred, or on Love ?
Since not Apostles' hands can clasp
Each other in so firm a grasp,
But they shall change and variance prove.

Yet deem not, on such parting sad
Shall dawn no welcome dear and glad :
Divided in their earthly race,
Together at the glorious goal,
Each leading many a rescu'd soul,
The faithful champions shall embrace.

For even as those mysterious Four,
Who the bright whirling wheels upbore
By Chebar in the fiery blast j,
So, on their tasks of love and praise
The saints of God their several ways
Right onward speed, yet join at last.

j They turned not when they went ; they went every one straight forward. *Ezekiel* i. 9.

And sometimes even beneath the moon
The Saviour gives a gracious boon,
  When reconciled Christians meet,
And face to face, and heart to heart,
High thoughts of holy love impart
  In silence meek, or converse sweet.

Companion of the Saints ! 'twas thine
To taste that drop of peace divine,
  When the great soldier of thy Lord
Call'd thee to take his last farewell,
Teaching the Church with joy to tell
  The story of your love restor'd.

O then the glory and the bliss,
When all that pain'd or seem'd amiss
  Shall melt with earth and sin away !
When saints beneath their Saviour's eye,
Fill'd with each other's company,
  Shall spend in love th' eternal day !

St. Philip and St. James.

Let the brother of low degree rejoice in that he is exalted: but the rich, in that he is made low. James i. 9, 10.

D EAR is the morning gale of spring,
    And dear th' autumnal eve;
But few delights can summer bring
    A Poet's crown to weave.

Her bowers are mute, her fountains dry,
    And ever Fancy's wing
Speeds from beneath her cloudless sky
    To autumn or to spring.

Sweet is the infant's waking smile,
    And sweet the old man's rest—
But middle age by no fond wile,
    No soothing calm is blest.

Still in the world's hot restless gleam
    She plies her weary task,
While vainly for some pleasant dream
    Her wandering glances ask.—

O shame upon thee, listless heart,
    So sad a sigh to heave,
As if thy Saviour had no part
    In thoughts, that make thee grieve.

As if along His lonesome way
    He had not borne for thee
Sad languors through the summer day,
    Storms on the wintry sea.

Youth's lightning flash of joy secure
    Pass'd seldom o'er His spright,—
A well of serious thought and pure,
    Too deep for earthly light.

No spring was His—no fairy gleam—
    For He by trial knew
How cold and bare what mortals dream,
    To worlds where all is true.

Then grudge not thou the anguish keen
    Which makes thee like thy Lord,
And learn to quit with eye serene
    Thy youth's ideal hoard.

Thy treasur'd hopes and raptures high—
    Unmurmuring let them go,
Nor grieve the bliss should quickly fly
    Which Christ disdain'd to know.

Thou shalt have joy in sadness soon ;
    The pure, calm hope be thine,
Which brightens, like the eastern moon,
    As day's wild lights decline.

Thus souls, by nature pitch'd too high,
    By sufferings plung'd too low,
Meet in the Church's middle sky,
    Half way 'twixt joy and woe,

To practise there the soothing lay
    That sorrow best relieves :
Thankful for all God takes away,
    Humbled by all He gives.

𝔖𝔱. 𝔅𝔞𝔯𝔫𝔞𝔟𝔞𝔰. *The son of consolation, a Levite.* Acts iv. 36.

THE world's a room of sickness, where each heart
    Knows its own anguish and unrest ;
The truest wisdom there, and noblest art,
    Is his, who skills of comfort best ;
Whom by the softest step and gentlest tone
    Enfeebled spirits own,
    And love to raise the languid eye,
When, like an angel's wing, they feel him fleeting by :—

Feel only—for in silence gently gliding
    Fain would he shun both ear and sight,
'Twixt Prayer and watchful Love his heart dividing,
    A nursing father day and night.
Such were the tender arms, where cradled lay,
    In her sweet natal day,
    The Church of Jesus ; such the love
He to his chosen taught for His dear widow'd Dove.

Warm'd underneath the Comforter's safe wing
    They spread th' endearing warmth around :
Mourners, speed here your broken hearts to bring,
    Here healing dews and balms abound :
Here are soft hands that cannot bless in vain,
    By trial taught your pain :
    Here loving hearts, that daily know
The heavenly consolations they on you bestow.

Sweet thoughts are theirs, that breathe serenest calms,
    Of holy offerings timely paid [k],

k Having land, sold it, and brought the money, and laid it at the
apostles' feet. *Acts* iv. 37.

Of fire from Heaven to bless their votive alms
    And passions on God's altar laid.
The world to them is clos'd, and now they shine
      With rays of love divine,
    Through darkest nooks of this dull earth
Pouring, in showery times, their glow of " quiet mirth."

New hearts before their Saviour's feet to lay,
    This is their first their dearest joy :
Their next, from heart to heart to clear the way [1]
    For mutual love without alloy :
    Never so blest, as when in Jesus' roll
      They write some hero-soul,
    More pleas'd upon his brightening road
To wait, than if their own with all his radiance glow'd.

O happy spirits, mark'd by God and man
    Their messages of love to bear [m],
What though long since in Heaven your brows began
    The genial amarant wreath to wear,
And in th' eternal leisure of calm love
      Ye banquet there above,
    Yet in your sympathetic heart
We and our earthly griefs may ask and hope a part.

Comfort's true sons ! amid the thoughts of down
    That strew your pillow of repose,
Sure, 'tis one joy to muse, how ye unknown
    By sweet remembrance soothe our woes,
And how the spark ye lit, of heavenly cheer
      Lives in our embers here,
    Where'er the Cross is borne with smiles,
Or lighten'd secretly by Love's endearing wiles :

[1] Barnabas took him, and brought him, Saul, to the apostles. *Acts* ix. 27.   [m] *Acts* xi. 22 : xiii. 2.

Where'er one Levite in the temple keeps
    The watch-fire of his.midnight prayer,
Or issuing thence, the eyes of mourners steeps
    In heavenly balm, fresh gather'd there ;
Thus saints, that seem to die in earth's rude strife,
    Only win double life :
    They have but left our weary ways
To live in memory here, in heaven by love and praise.

St. John Baptist's Day.

Behold, I will send you Elijah the prophet before the coming of the great and dreadful day of the Lord : and he shall turn the heart of the fathers to the children, and the heart of the children to their fathers. Malachi iv. 5, 6.

T WICE in her season of decay
  The fallen Church hath felt Elijah's eye
 Dart from the wild its piercing ray :
Not keener burns, in the chill morning sky,
   The herald star,
   Whose torch afar
 Shadows and boding night-birds fly.

  Methinks we need him once again,
That favour'd seer—but where shall he be found ?
 By Cherith's side we seek in vain,
In vain on Carmel's green and lonely mound :
   Angels no more
   From Sinai soar,
 On his celestial errands bound.

  But wafted to her glorious place
By harmless fire, among the ethereal thrones,
 His spirit with a dear embrace
Thee the lov'd harbinger of Jesus owns,
   Well-pleas'd to view
   Her likeness true,
 And trace, in thine, her own deep tones.

  Deathless himself, he joys with thee
To commune how a faithful martyr dies,

And in the blest could envy be,
He would behold thy wounds with envious eyes,
  Star of our morn,
  Who yet unborn [n]
Didst guide our hope, where Christ should rise.

  Now resting from your jealous care
For sinners, such as Eden cannot know,
  Ye pour for us your mingled prayer,
No anxious fear to damp Affection's glow,
  Love draws a cloud
  From you to shroud
Rebellion's mystery here below.

  And since we see, and not afar,
The twilight of the great and dreadful day,
  Why linger, till Elijah's car
Stoop from the clouds? Why sleep ye? rise and pray,
  Ye heralds seal'd
  In camp or field
Your Saviour's banner to display.

  Where is the lore the Baptist taught,
The soul unswerving and the fearless tongue?
  The much-enduring wisdom, sought
By lonely prayer the haunted rocks among?
  Who counts it gain [o]
  His light should wane,
So the whole world to Jesus throng?

  Thou Spirit who the Church didst lend
Her eagle wings, to shelter in the wild [p],
  We pray thee, ere the Judge descend,

n The babe leaped in my womb for joy. *St. Luke* i. 44.
o He must increase, but I must decrease. *St. John* iii. 30.
p Revelations xii. 14.

With flames like these, all bright and undefil'd,
  Her watchfires light,
  To guide aright
Our weary souls, by earth beguil'd.

  So glorious let thy Pastors shine,
That by their speaking lives the world may learn
  First filial duty, then divine q,
That sons to parents, all to Thee may turn ;
  And ready prove
  In fires of love,
At sight of Thee, for aye to burn.

q He shall turn the heart of the fathers to the children, and the
heart of the children to their fathers. *Malachi* iv. 6.
 To turn the hearts of the fathers to the children, and the disobedient
to the wisdom of the just ; to make ready a people prepared for the
Lord. *St. Luke* i. 17.

St. Peter's Day.

When Herod would have brought him forth, the same night Peter was sleeping. Acts xii. 6.

THOU thrice denied, yet thrice belov'd [r],
    Watch by thine own forgiven friend ;
In sharpest perils faithful prov'd,
    Let his soul love thee to the end.

The prayer is heard—else why so deep
    His slumber on the eve of death?
And wherefore smiles he in his sleep
    As one who drew celestial breath?

He loves and is belov'd again—
    Can his soul choose but be at rest ?
Sorrow hath fled away, and Pain
    Dares not invade the guarded nest.

He dearly loves, and not alone :
    For his wing'd thoughts are soaring high
Where never yet frail heart was known
    To breathe in vain affection's sigh.

He loves and weeps—but more than tears
    Have seal'd thy welcome and his love—
One look lives in him, and endears
    Crosses and wrongs where'er he rove :

That gracious chiding look [s], Thy call
    To win him to himself and Thee,

[r] St. John xxi. 15—17.   [s] St. Luke xxii. 61.

Sweetening the sorrow of his fall
  Which else were ru'd too bitterly.

Even through the veil of sleep it shines,
  The memory of that kindly glance ;—
The Angel watching by divines
  And spares awhile his blissful trance.

Or haply to his native lake
  His vision wafts him back, to talk
With Jesus, ere his flight he take,
  As in that solemn evening walk,

When to the bosom of his friend,
  The Shepherd, He whose name is Good,
Did His dear lambs and sheep commend,
  Both bought and nourish'd with His blood :

Then laid on him th' inverted tree,
  Which firm embrac'd with heart and arm,
Might cast o'er hope and memory,
  O'er life and death, its awful charm.

With brightening heart he bears it on,
  His passport thro' th' eternal gates,
To his sweet home—so nearly won,
  He seems, as by the door he waits,

The unexpressive notes to hear
  Of angel song and angel motion,
Rising and falling on the ear
  Like waves in Joy's unbounded ocean.

His dream is chang'd—the Tyrant's voice
  Calls to that last of glorious deeds—

But as he rises to rejoice,
  Not Herod but an Angel leads.

He dreams he sees a lamp flash bright,
  Glancing around his prison room—
But 'tis a gleam of heavenly light
  That fills up all the ample gloom.

The flame, that in a few short years
  Deep through the chambers of the dead
Shall pierce, and dry the fount of tears,
  Is waving o'er his dungeon-bed.

Touch'd he upstarts—his chains unbind—
  Through darksome vault, up massy stair,
His dizzy, doubting footsteps wind
  To freedom and cool moonlight air.

Then all himself, all joy and calm,
  Though for a while his hand forego,
Just as it touch'd, the martyr's palm,
  He turns him to his task below ;

The pastoral staff, the keys of heaven,
  To wield awhile in grey-hair'd might,
Then from his cross to spring forgiven,
  And follow Jesus out of sight.

St. James's Day.

*Ye shall drink indeed of my cup, and be
baptized with the baptism that I am
baptized with: but to sit on my right
hand, and on my left, is not mine to
give, but it shall be given to them for
whom it is prepared of my Father.*

St. Matthew xx. 23.

S IT down and take thy fill of joy
    At God's right hand, a bidden guest,
Drink of the cup that cannot cloy,
    Eat of the bread that cannot waste.
O great Apostle ! rightly now
    Thou readest all thy Saviour meant,
What time His grave yet gentle brow
    In sweet reproof on thee was bent.

" Seek ye to sit enthron'd by me ?
    " Alas ! ye know not what ye ask,
" The first in shame and agony,
    " The lowest in the meanest task—
" This can ye be? and can ye drink
    " The cup that I in tears must steep,
" Nor from the whelming waters shrink
    " That o'er me roll so dark and deep ? "

" We can—thine are we, dearest Lord,
    " In glory and in agony,
" To do and suffer all Thy word ;
    " Only be Thou for ever nigh :"
" Then be it so—my cup receive,
    " And of my woes baptismal taste :

" But for the crown, that angels weave
  " For those next me in glory plac'd,

" I give it not by partial love ;
  " But in my Father's book are writ
" What names on earth shall lowliest prove,
  " That they in Heaven may highest sit."
Take up the lesson, O my heart ;
  Thou Lord of meekness, write it there,
Thine own meek self to me impart,
  Thy lofty hope, thy lowly prayer :

If ever on the mount with Thee
  I seem to soar in vision bright,
With thoughts of coming agony [t],
  Stay Thou the too presumptuous flight :
Gently along the vale of tears
  Lead me from Tabor's sunbright steep,
Let me not grudge a few short years
  With Thee tow'rd Heaven to walk and weep :

Too happy, on my silent path,
  If now and then allow'd, with Thee
Watching some placid holy death,
  Thy secret work of love to see ;
But oh most happy, should thy call,
  Thy welcome call, at last be given—
" Come where thou long hast stor'd thy all,
  " Come see thy place prepar'd in Heaven."

[t] *St. Matthew* xvii. 12. " Likewise shall also the Son of man suffer of them." This was just after the Transfiguration.

St. Bartholo-mew.

Jesus answered and said unto him, Because I said unto thee, I saw thee under the fig tree, believest thou? thou shalt see greater things than these.
St. John i. 50.

H OLD up thy mirror to the sun,
　And thou shalt need an eagle's gaze,
So perfectly the polish'd stone
　Gives back the glory of his rays :

Turn it, and it shall paint as true
　The soft green of the vernal earth,
And each small flower of bashful hue,
　That closest hides its lowly birth.

Our mirror is a blessed book,
　Where out from each illumin'd page
We see one glorious Image look
　All eyes to dazzle and engage,

The Son of God : and that indeed
　We see Him, as He is, we know,
Since in the same bright glass we read
　The very life of things below.—

Eye of God's word [u] ! where'er we turn
　Ever upon us ! thy keen gaze

[u] " The position before us is, that we ourselves, and such as we, are the very persons whom Scripture speaks of: and to whom, as men, in every variety of persuasive form, it makes its condescending though celestial appeal.　The point worthy of observation is, to note how a book of the description and the compass which we have represented Scripture to be, possesses this versatility of power ; *this eye, like that of a portrait, uniformly fixed upon us, turn where we will.*" Miller's Bampton Lectures, p. 128.

Can all the depths of sin discern,
　　Unravel every bosom's maze :

Who that has felt thy glance of dread
　　Thrill through his heart's remotest cells,
About his path, about his bed,
　　Can doubt what spirit in thee dwells ?

" What word is this ? Whence know'st thou me ?"
　　All wondering cries the humbled heart,
To hear thee that deep mystery,
　　The knowledge of itself, impart.

The veil is rais'd ; who runs may read,
　　By its own light the truth is seen,
And soon the Israelite indeed
　　Bows down t' adore the Nazarene.

So did Nathanael, guileless man,
　　At once, not shame-fac'd or afraid,
Owning him God, who so could scan
　　His musings in the lonely shade ;

In his own pleasant fig-tree's shade,
　　Which by his household fountain grew,
Where at noon-day his prayer he made,
　　To know God better than he knew.

Oh ! happy hours of heav'n-ward thought !
　　How richly crown'd ! how well improv'd !
In musing o'er the Law he taught,
　　In waiting for the Lord he lov'd.

We must not mar with earthly praise
　　What God's approving word hath seal'd ;
Enough, if right our feeble lays
　　Take up the promise He reveal'd ;

" The child-like faith, that asks not sight,
  " Waits not for wonder or for sign,
" Believes, because it loves, aright—
  " Shall see things greater, things divine.

" Heaven to that gaze shall open wide,
  " And brightest angels to and fro
" On messages of love shall glide
  " 'Twixt God above, and Christ below."

So still the guileless man is blest,
  To him all crooked paths are straight,
Him on his way to endless rest
  Fresh, ever-growing strengths await ^v.

God's witnesses, a glorious host,
  Compass him daily like a cloud ;
Martyrs and seers, the sav'd and lost,
  Mercies and judgments cry aloud.

Yet shall to him the still small voice,
  That first into his bosom found
A way, and fix'd his wavering choice,
  Nearest and dearest ever sound.

^v They go from strength to strength. *Psalm* lxxxiv. 7.

St. Matthew.

And after these things he went forth, and saw a publican, named Levi, sitting at the receipt of custom : and he said unto him, Follow me. And he left all, rose up, and followed him. St. Luke v. 27, 28.

Y E hermits blest, ye holy maids,
　　The nearest heaven on earth,
Who talk with God in shadowy glades,
　　Free from rude care and mirth ;
To whom some viewless teacher brings
The secret lore of rural things,
The moral of each fleeting cloud and gale,
The whispers from above, that haunt the twilight vale :

　　Say, when in pity ye have gaz'd
　　　　On the wreath'd smoke afar,
　　That o'er some town, like mist uprais'd,
　　　　Hung hiding sun and star,
　　Then as ye turn'd your weary eye
　　To the green earth and open sky,
　Were ye not fain to doubt how Faith could dwell
Amid that dreary glare, in this world's citadel ?

　　But Love's a flower that will not die
　　　　For lack of leafy screen,
　　And Christian Hope can cheer the eye
　　　　That ne'er saw vernal green ;
　　Then be ye sure that Love can bless
　　Even in this crowded loneliness,
　Where ever-moving myriads seem to say,
Go—thou art nought to us, nor we to thee—away !

There are in this loud stunning tide
 Of human care and crime,
With whom the melodies abide
 Of th' everlasting chime ;
Who carry music in their heart
Through dusky lane and wrangling mart,
Plying their daily task with busier feet,
Because their secret souls a holy strain repeat.

How sweet to them, in such brief rest
 As thronging cares afford,
In thought to wander, fancy-blest,
 To where their gracious Lord,
In vain, to win proud Pharisees,
Spake, and was heard by fell disease [x]—
But not in vain, beside yon breezy lake,
Bade the meek Publican his gainful seat forsake :

At once he rose, and left his gold,
 His treasure and his heart
Transferr'd, where he shall safe behold
 Earth and her idols part ;
While he beside his endless store
Shall sit, and floods unceasing pour
Of Christ's true riches o'er all time and space,
First angel of his Church, first steward of his Grace.

Nor can ye not delight to think [y]
 Where He vouchsaf'd to eat,
How the Most Holy did not shrink
 From touch of sinner's meat ;
What worldly hearts and hearts impure
Went with him through the rich man's door,

[x] It seems from St. Matthew ix. 8, 9, that the calling of Levi took place immediately after the healing of the paralytic in the presence of the Pharisees. [y] St. Matthew ix. 10.

That we might learn of Him lost souls to love,
And view his least and worst with hope to meet above.

    These gracious lines shed Gospel light
      On Mammon's gloomiest cells,
    As on some city's cheerless night
      The tide of sun-rise swells,
    Till tower, and dome, and bridge-way proud
    Are mantled with a golden cloud,
  And to wise hearts this certain hope is given ;
" No mist that man may raise, shall hide the eye of
      " Heaven."

    And oh ! if even on Babel shine
      Such gleams of Paradise,
    Should not their peace be peace divine,
      Who day by day arise
    To look on clearer Heavens, and scan
    The work of God untouch'd by man ?
  Shame on us, who about us Babel bear,
And live in Paradise, as if God was not there !

St. Michael and all Angels.

Y E stars that round the Sun of righteousness
    In glorious order roll,
With harps for ever strung, ready to bless
    God for each rescued soul,
Ye eagle spirits, that build in light divine,
    Oh think of us to-day,
Faint warblers of this earth, that would combine
Our trembling notes with your accepted lay.

Your amarant wreaths were earn'd ; and homeward all,
    Flush'd with victorious might,
Ye might have sped to keep high festival,
    And revel in the light ;
But meeting us, weak worldlings, on our way,
    Tired ere the fight begun,
Ye turn'd to help us in th' unequal fray,
Remembering whose we were, how dearly won :

Remembering Bethlehem, and that glorious night
    When ye, who used to soar
Diverse along all space in fiery flight,
    Came thronging to adore
Your God new-born, and made a sinner's child ;
    As if the stars should leave
Their stations in the far ethereal wild,
And round the sun a radiant circle weave.

Nor less your lay of triumph greeted fair
    Our Champion and your King,

17

In that first strife, whence Satan in despair
        Sunk down on scathed wing :
Alone He fasted, and alone He fought ;
        But when his toils were o'er,
Ye to the sacred Hermit duteous brought
Banquet and hymn, your Eden's festal store.

Ye too, when lowest in th' abyss of woe
        He plung'd to save his sheep,
Were leaning from your golden thrones to know
        The secrets of that deep :
But clouds were on his sorrow : one alone
        His agonizing call
Summon'd from Heaven, to still that bitterest groan,
And comfort Him, the Comforter of all.

Oh ! highest favour'd of all Spirits create,
        If right of thee we deem,
How didst thou glide on brightening wing elate
        To meet th' unclouded beam
Of Jesus from the couch of darkness rising !
        How swell'd thine anthem's sound,
With fear and mightier joy weak hearts surprising,
" Your God is risen, and may not here be found !"

Pass a few days, and this dull darkling globe
        Must yield him from her sight ;—
Brighter and brighter streams his glory-robe,
        And He is lost in light.
Then, when through yonder everlasting arch,
        Ye in innumerous choir
Pour'd, heralding Messiah's conquering march,
Linger'd around his skirts two forms of fire :

With us they staid, high warning to impart ;
        " The Christ shall come again

" Even as He goes ; with the same human heart,
    " With the same godlike train."—
Oh ! jealous God ! how could a sinner dare
    Think on that dreadful day,
But that with all thy wounds Thou wilt be there,
And all our angel friends to bring Thee on thy way?

Since to thy little ones is given such grace,
    That they who nearest stand
Alway to God in Heaven, and see His face,
    Go forth at his command,
To wait around our path in weal or woe,
    As erst upon our King,
Set thy baptismal seal upon our brow,
And waft us heaven-ward with enfolding wing :

Grant, Lord, that when around th' expiring world
    Our Seraph guardians wait,
While on her death-bed, ere to ruin hurl'd,
    She owns thee, all too late,
They to their charge may turn, and thankful see
    Thy mark upon us still ;
Then all together rise, and reign with Thee,
And all their holy joy o'er contrite hearts fulfil !

St. Luke.

Luke, the beloved physician, and Demas, greet you. Colossians iv. 14.
Demas hath forsaken me, having loved this present world . . Only Luke is with me.
2 Timothy iv. 10, 11.

T WO clouds before the summer gale
  In equal race fleet o'er the sky :
Two flowers, when wintry blasts assail,
  Together pine, together die.

But two capricious human hearts—
  No sage's rod may track their ways,
No eye pursue their lawless starts
  Along their wild self-chosen maze.

He only, by whose sovereign hand
  Even sinners for the evil day [z]
Were made—who rules the world he plann'd,
  Turning our worst his own good way ;

He only can the cause reveal,
  Why, at the same fond bosom fed,
Taught in the self-same lap to kneel
  Till the same prayer were duly said,

Brothers in blood and nurture too,
  Aliens in heart so oft should prove ;
One lose, the other keep, Heaven's clue ;
  One dwell in wrath, and one in love.

[z] The Lord hath made all things for himself: yea, even the wicked for the day of evil. *Proverbs* xvi. 4.

He only knows,—for He can read
　The mystery of the wicked heart,—
Why vainly oft our arrows speed
　When aim'd with most unerring art ;

While from some rude and powerless arm
　A random shaft in season sent
Shall light upon some lurking harm,
　And work some wonder little meant.

Doubt we, how souls so wanton change,
　Leaving their own experienc'd rest ?
Needs not around the world to range ;
　One narrow cell may teach us best.

Look in, and see Christ's chosen saint
　In triumph wear his Christ-like chain ;
No fear lest he should swerve or faint ;
　" His life is Christ, his death is gain [a]."

Two converts, watching by his side,
　Alike his love and greetings share ;
Luke the belov'd, the sick soul's guide,
　And Demas, nam'd in faltering prayer.

Pass a few years—look in once more—
　The saint is in his bonds again ;
Save that his hopes more boldly soar [b],
　He and his lot unchang'd remain.

But only Luke is with him now :—
　Alas ! that even the martyr's cell,

[a] Philippians i. 21.
[b] In the Epistle to the Philippians, "I know that I shall abide
and continue with you all . . . . I count not myself to have appre-
hended." Chap. i. 25 ; iii. 13.
In 2 Timothy, "I have finished my course," etc. ch. iv. 7. 8.

Heaven's very gate, should scope al'ow
   For the false world's seducing spell.

'Tis sad—but yet 'tis well, be sure,
   We on the sight should muse awhile,
Nor deem our shelter all secure
   Even in the Church's holiest aisle.

Vainly before the shrine he bends,
   Who knows not the true pilgrim's part :
The martyr's cell no safety lends
   To him, who wants the martyr's heart.

But if there be, who follows Paul
   As Paul his Lord, in life and death,
Where'er an aching heart may call,
   Ready to speed and take no breath ;

Whose joy is, to the wandering sheep
   To tell of the great Shepherd's love [c];
To learn of mourners while they weep
   The music that makes mirth above ;

Who makes the Saviour all his theme,
   The Gospel all his pride and praise—
Approach : for thou canst feel the gleam
   That round the martyr's death-bed plays :

Thou hast an ear for angels' songs,
   A breath the Gospel trump to fill,
And taught by thee the Church prolongs
   Her hymns of high thanksgiving still [d].

[c] The Gospel of St. Luke abounds most in such passages as the parable of the lost sheep, which display God's mercy to penitent sinners.

[d] The Christian hymns are all in St. Luke : the Magnificat, Benedictus, and Nunc Dimittis.

Ah! dearest mother, since too oft
    The world yet wins some Demas frail
Even from thine arms, so kind and soft,
    May thy tried comforts never fail !

When faithless ones forsake thy wing,
    Be it vouchsaf'd thee still to see
Thy true, fond nurslings closer cling,
    Cling closer to their Lord and thee.

St. Simon and St. Jude.

That ye should earnestly contend for (•) the faith which was once delivered unto the saints. St. Jude 3.

SEEST thou, how tearful and alone,
  And drooping like a wounded dove,
The Cross in sight, but Jesus gone,
  The widow'd Church is fain to rove?

Who is at hand that loves the Lord [f]?
  Make haste and take her home, and bring
Thine household choir, in true accord
  Their soothing hymns for her to sing.

Soft on her fluttering heart shall breathe
  The fragrance of that genial isle,
There she may weave her funeral wreath,
  And to her own sad music smile.

The Spirit of the dying Son
  Is there, and fills the holy place
With records sweet of duties done,
  Of pardon'd foes, and cherish'd grace.

And as of old by two and two [g]
  His herald saints the Saviour sent
To soften hearts like morning dew,
  Where He to shine in mercy meant;

[e] ἐπαγωνίζεσθαι : "be very anxious for it:" "feel for it as for a friend in jeopardy."
[f] Then saith he to the disciple, Behold thy mother! And from that hour that disciple took her unto his own home. *St. John* xix. 27.
[g] St. Mark vi. 7 ; St. Luke x. 1.

So evermore He deems his name
    Best honour'd and His way prepar'd,
When watching by his altar flame
    He sees his servants duly pair'd.

He loves when age and youth are met,
    Fervent old age and youth serene,
Their high and low in concord set
    For sacred song, Joy's golden mean.

He loves when some clear soaring mind
    Is drawn by mutual piety
To simple souls and unrefin'd,
    Who in life's shadiest covert lie.

Or if perchance a sadden'd heart
    That once was gay and felt the spring,
Cons slowly o'er its alter'd part,
    In sorrow and remorse to sing,

Thy gracious care will send that way
    Some spirit full of glee, yet taught
To bear the sight of dull decay,
    And nurse it with all pitying thought ;

Cheerful as soaring lark, and mild
    As evening blackbird's full-ton'd lay,
When the relenting sun has smil'd
    Bright through a whole December day.

These are the tones to brace and cheer
    The lonely watcher of the fold,
When nights are dark, and foemen near,
    When visions fade and hearts grow cold.

How timely then a comrade's song
    Comes floating on the mountain air,
And bids thee yet be bold and strong—
    Fancy may die, but Faith is there.

All Saints' Day.

WHY blow'st thou not, thou wintry wind,
　　Now every leaf is brown and sere,
And idly droops, to thee resign'd,
　　The fading chaplet of the year?
Yet wears the pure aerial sky
Her summer veil, half drawn on high,
Of silvery haze; and dark and still
The shadows sleep on every slanting hill.

How quiet shews the woodland scene!
　　Each flower and tree, its duty done,
Reposing in decay serene,
　　Like weary men when age is won,
Such calm old age as conscience pure
And self-commanding hearts ensure,
Waiting their summons to the sky,
Content to live, but not afraid to die.

Sure if our eyes were purg'd to trace
　　God's unseen armies hovering round,
We should behold by angels' grace
　　The four strong winds of Heaven fast bound,
Their downward sweep a moment staid
On ocean cove and forest glade,
Till the last flower of autumn shed
Her funeral odours on her dying bed.

So in thine awful armoury, Lord,
  The lightnings of the judgment day
Pause yet awhile, in mercy stor'd,
  Till willing hearts wear quite away
Their earthly stains ; and spotless shine
On every brow in light divine
The Cross by angel hands impress'd,
The seal of glory won and pledge of promis'd rest.

Little they dream, those haughty souls
  Whom empires own with bended knee,
What lowly fate their own controuls,
  Together link'd by Heaven's decree ;—
As bloodhounds hush their baying wild
To wanton with some fearless child,
So Famine waits, and War with greedy eyes,
Till some repenting heart be ready for the skies.

Think ye the spires that glow so bright
  In front of yonder setting sun,
Stand by their own unshaken might ?
  No—where th' upholding grace is won,
We dare not ask, nor Heaven would tell,
But sure from many a hidden dell,
From many a rural nook unthought of there,
Rises for that proud world the saints' prevailing prayer.

On champions blest, in Jesus' name,
  Short be your strife, your triumph full,
Till every heart have caught your flame,
  And lighten'd of the world's misrule,
Ye soar those elder saints to meet,
Gather'd long since at Jesus' feet,
No world of passions to destroy,
Your prayers and struggles o'er, your task all praise
    and joy.

Holy Communion.

O GOD of Mercy, God of Might,
　　How should pale sinners bear the sight,
If, as Thy power is surely here,
Thine open glory should appear?

For now thy people are allow'd
To scale the mount and pierce the cloud,
And Faith may feed her eager view
With wonders Sinai never knew.

Fresh from th' atoning sacrifice
The world's Creator bleeding lies,
That man, his foe, by whom He bled,
May take him for his daily bread.

O agony of wavering thought
When sinners first so near are brought!
" It is my Maker—dare I stay?
" My Saviour—dare I turn away?"

Thus while the storm is high within
'Twixt love of Christ and fear of sin,
Who can express the soothing charm,
To feel thy kind upholding arm,

My mother Church? and hear thee tell
Of a world lost, yet lov'd so well,
That He, by whom the angels live,
His only Son for her would give [h].

[h] " God so loved the world, that He gave His only-begotten Son."
See the sentences in the Communion Service, after the Confession.

And doubt we yet? thou call'st again;
A lower still, a sweeter strain;
A voice from Mercy's inmost shrine,
The very breath of Love divine.

Whispering it says to each apart,
" Come unto me, thou trembling heart [i] ;"
And we must hope, so sweet the tone,
The precious words are all our own.

Hear them, kind Saviour—hear thy spouse
Low at thy feet renew her vows;
Thine own dear promise she would plead
For us her true though fallen seed.

She pleads by all thy mercies, told
Thy chosen witnesses of old,
Love's heralds sent to man forgiven,
One from the Cross, and one from heaven [j].

This, of true Penitents the chief,
To the lost spirit brings relief,
Lifting on high th' adored name :—
" Sinners to save, Christ Jesus came [k]."

That, dearest of thy bosom Friends,
Into the wavering heart descends :—
" What? fall'n again? yet cheerful rise [l],
" Thine Intercessor never dies."

The eye of Faith, that waxes bright
Each moment by thine altar's light,

[i] Come unto Me all ye that travail and are heavy laden, and I will refresh you.   [j] St. Paul and St. John.

[k] This is a faithful saying and worthy of all men to be received, That Christ Jesus came into the world to save sinners.

[l] If any man sin, we have an Advocate with the Father, Jesus Christ the righteous.

Sees them e'en now : they still abide
In mystery kneeling at our side ;

And with them every spirit blest,
From realms of triumph or of rest,
From Him who saw creation's morn,
Of all thine angels eldest born,

To the poor babe, who died to-day,
Take part in our thanksgiving lay,
Watching the tearful joy and calm,
While sinners taste thine heavenly balm.

Sweet awful hour ! the only sound
One gentle footstep gliding round,
Offering by turns on Jesus' part
The Cross to every hand and heart.

Refresh us, Lord, to hold it fast ;
And when thy veil is drawn at last,
Let us depart where shadows cease,
With words of blessing and of peace.

Holy Baptism.

W HERE is it, mothers learn their love?—
In every Church a fountain springs
O'er which th' eternal Dove
Hovers on softest wings.

What sparkles in that lucid flood
Is water, by gross mortals ey'd:
But seen by Faith, 'tis blood
Out of a dear friend's side.

A few calm words of faith and prayer,
A few bright drops of holy dew,
Shall work a wonder there
Earth's charmers never knew.

O happy arms, where cradled lies,
And ready for the Lord's embrace,
That precious sacrifice,
The darling of his grace!

Blest eyes, that see the smiling gleam
Upon the slumbering features glow,
When the life-giving stream
Touches the tender brow!

Or when the holy cross is sign'd,
And the young soldier duly sworn
With true and fearless mind
To serve the Virgin-born.

But happiest ye, who seal'd and blest
Back to your arms your treasure take,

With Jesus' mark impress'd
To nurse for Jesus' sake :

To whom—as if in hallow'd air
Ye knelt before some awful shrine—
His innocent gestures wear
A meaning half divine :

By whom Love's daily touch is seen
In strengthening form and freshening hue,
In the fix'd brow serene,
The deep yet eager view.—

Who taught thy pure and even breath
To come and go with such sweet grace?
Whence thy reposing Faith,
Though in our frail embrace?

O tender gem, and full of Heaven !
Not in the twilight stars on high
Not in moist flowers at even
See we our God so nigh.

Sweet one, make haste and know Him too,
Thine own adopting Father love,
That like thine earliest dew
Thy dying sweets may prove.

Catechism.

OH say not, dream not, heavenly notes
    To childish ears are vain,
That the young mind at random floats,
    And cannot reach the strain.

Dim or unheard, the words may fall,
    And yet the heaven-taught mind
May learn the sacred air, and all
    The harmony unwind.

Was not our Lord a little child,
    Taught by degrees to pray,
By father dear and mother mild
    Instructed day by day?

And lov'd He not of Heaven to talk
    With children in His sight,
To meet them in His daily walk,
    And to His arms invite?

What though around His throne of fire
    The everlasting chant
Be wafted from the seraph choir
    In glory jubilant!

Yet stoops He, ever pleas'd to mark
    Our rude essays of love,
Faint as the pipe of wakening lark,
    Heard by some twilight grove:

18

Yet is He near us, to survey
　　These bright and order'd files,
Like spring-flowers in their best array,
　　All silence and all smiles,

Save that each little voice in turn
　　Some glorious truth proclaims,
What sages would have died to learn,
　　Now taught by cottage dames.

And if some tones be false or low,
　　What are all prayers beneath
But cries of babes, that cannot know
　　Half the deep thought they breathe?

In His own words we Christ adore,
　　But angels, as we speak,
Higher above our meaning soar
　　Than we o'er children weak:

And yet His words mean more than they,
　　And yet He owns their praise:
Why should we think, He turns away
　　From infants' simple lays?

Confirmation.

THE shadow of th' Almighty's cloud
   Calm on the tents of Israel lay,
While drooping paus'd twelve banners proud,
   Till He arise and lead the way.

Then to the desert breeze unroll'd
   Cheerly the waving pennons fly,
Lion or eagle—each bright fold
   A loadstar to a warrior's eye.

So should thy champions, ere the strife,
   By holy hands o'er-shadow'd kneel,
So, fearless for their charmed life,
   Bear, to the end, thy Spirit's seal.

Steady and pure as stars that beam
   In middle heaven, all mist above,
Seen deepest in the frozen stream :—
   Such is their high courageous love.

And soft as pure, and warm as bright,
   They brood upon life's peaceful hour,
As if the Dove that guides their flight
   Shook from her plumes a downy shower.

Spirit of might and sweetness too !
   Now leading on the wars of God,
Now to green isles of shade and dew
   Turning the waste thy people trod ;

Draw, Holy Ghost, thy seven-fold veil
   Between us and the fires of youth ;

Breathe, Holy Ghost, thy freshening gale,
   Our fever'd brow in age to soothe.

And oft as sin and sorrow tire
   The hallow'd hour do Thou renew
When beckon'd up the awful choir
   By pastoral hands, toward Thee we drew;

When trembling at the sacred rail
   We hid our eyes, and held our breath,
Felt thee how strong, our hearts how frail,
   And long'd to own thee to the death.

For ever on our souls be trac'd
   That blessing dear, that dove-like hand,
A sheltering rock in Memory's waste,
   O'er-shadowing all the weary land.

Matrimony.

THERE is an awe in mortals' joy,
  A deep mysterious fear
Half of the heart will still employ,
  As if we drew too near
To Eden's portal, and those fires
That bicker round in wavy spires,
Forbidding, to our frail desires,
  What cost us once so dear.

We cower before th' heart-searching eye
  In rapture as in pain;
Even wedded Love, till thou be nigh,
  Dares not believe her gain :
Then in the air she fearless springs,
The breath of Heaven beneath her wings,
And leaves her woodnote wild, and sings
  A tun'd and measur'd strain.

Ill fare the lay, though soft as dew
  And free as air it fall,
That, with thine altar full in view,
  Thy votaries would enthrall
To a foul dream, of heathen night,
Lifting her torch in Love's despite,
And scaring with base wildfire light
  The sacred nuptial hall.

Far other strains, far other fires,
  Our marriage offering grace ;
Welcome, all chaste and kind desires,
  With even matron pace

Approaching down the hallow'd aisle !
Where should ye seek Love's perfect smile,
But where your prayers were learn'd erewhile,
    In her own native place?

Where, but on His benignest brow,
    Who waits to bless you here?
Living, He own'd no nuptial vow,
    No bower to Fancy dear :
Love's very self—for Him no need
To nurse, on earth, the heavenly seed :
Yet comfort in His eye we read
    For bridal joy and fear.

'Tis He who clasps the marriage band,
    And fits the spousal ring,
Then leaves ye kneeling, hand in hand,
    Out of His stores to bring
His Father's dearest blessing, shed
Of old on Isaac's nuptial bed,
Now on the board before ye spread
    Of our all-bounteous King.

All blessings of the breast and womb,
    Of heaven and earth beneath,
Of converse high, and sacred home,
    Are yours, in life and death.
Only kneel on, nor turn away
From the pure shrine, where Christ to-day
Will store each flower, ye duteous lay,
    For an eternal wreath.

Visitation and Communion of the Sick.

O YOUTH and Joy, your airy tread
    Too lightly springs by Sorrow's bed,
Your keen eye glances are too bright,
Too restless for a sick man's sight.
Farewell ; for one short life we part :
I rather woo the soothing art,
Which only souls in sufferings tried
Bear to their suffering brethren's side.

Where may we learn that gentle spell ?
Mother of Martyrs, thou canst tell !
Thou, who didst watch thy dying Spouse
With pierced hands and bleeding brows,
Whose tears from age to age are shed
O'er sainted sons untimely dead,
If e'er we charm a soul in pain,
Thine is the key-note of our strain.

How sweet with thee to lift the latch,
Where Faith has kept her midnight watch,
Smiling on woe : with thee to kneel,
Where fix'd, as if one prayer could heal,
She listens, till her pale eye glow
With joy, wild health can never know,
And each calm feature, ere we read
Speaks, silently, thy glorious Creed.

Such have I seen : and while they pour'd
Their hearts in every contrite word,

How have I rather long'd to kneel
And ask of them sweet pardon's seal !
How blest the heavenly music brought
By thee to aid my faltering thought !
Peace ere we kneel, and when we cease
To pray, the farewell word is, " Peace."

I came again : the place was bright
" With something of celestial light"—
A simple altar by the bed
For high Communion meetly spread,
Chalice, and plate, and snowy vest.—
We ate and drank : then calmly blest,
All mourners, one with dying breath,
We sate and talk'd of Jesus' death.

Once more I came : the silent room
Was veil'd in sadly-soothing gloom,
And ready for her last abode
The pale form like a lily shew'd,
By virgin fingers duly spread,
And priz'd for love of summer fled.
The light from those soft-smiling eyes
Had fleeted to its parent skies.

O soothe us, haunt us, night and day,
Ye gentle Spirits far away,
With whom we shar'd the cup of grace,
Then parted ; ye to Christ's embrace,
We to the lonesome world again,
Yet mindful of th' unearthly strain
Practis'd with you at Eden's door,
To be sung on, where angels soar,
With blended voices evermore.

Burial of the Dead.

And when the Lord saw her, he had compassion on her, and said unto her, Weep not. And he came and touched the bier: and they that bare him stood still. And he said, Young man, I say unto thee, Arise. St. Luke vii. 13, 14.

WHO says, the wan autumnal sun
    Beams with too faint a smile
To light up nature's face again,
And, though the year be on the wane,
    With thoughts of spring the heart beguile?

Waft him, thou soft September breeze,
    And gently lay him down
Within some circling woodland wall,
Where bright leaves, reddening ere they fall,
    Wave gaily o'er the waters brown.

And let some graceful arch be there
    With wreathed mullions proud,
With burnish'd ivy for its screen,
And moss, that glows as fresh and green
    As though beneath an April cloud.—

Who says the widow's heart must break,
    The childless mother sink?—
A kinder truer voice I hear,
Which even beside that mournful bier
    Whence parents' eyes would hopeless shrink,

Bids weep no more—O heart bereft,
    How strange, to thee, that sound!

A widow o'er her only son,
Feeling more bitterly alone
   For friends that press officious round.

Yet is the voice of comfort heard,
   For Christ hath touch'd the bier—
The bearers wait with wondering eye,
The swelling bosom dares not sigh,
   But all is still, 'twixt hope and fear.

Even such an awful soothing calm
   We sometimes see alight
On Christian mourners, while they wait
In silence, by some church-yard gate, ·
   Their summons to the holy rite.

And such the tones of love, which break
   The stillness of that hour,
Quelling th' embitter'd spirit's strife—
" The Resurrection and the Life
   " Am I : believe, and die no more."—

Unchang'd that voice—and though not yet
   The dead sit up and speak,
Answering its call ; we gladlier rest
Our darlings on earth's quiet breast,
   And our hearts feel they must not break.

Far better they should sleep awhile
   Within the church's shade,
Nor wake, until new heaven, new earth,
Meet for their new immortal birth
   For their abiding-place be made,

Than wander back to life, and lean
   On our frail love once more.

Tis sweet, as year by year we lose
Friends out of sight, in faith to muse
   How grows in Paradise our store.

Then pass, ye mourners, cheerly on,
   Through prayer unto the tomb,
Still, as ye watch life's falling leaf,
Gathering from every loss and grief
   Hope of new spring and endless home.

Then cheerly to your work again
   With hearts new-brac'd and set
To run, untir'd, love's blessed race,
As meet for those, who face to face
   Over the grave their Lord have met.

Churching of Women.

IS there, in bowers of endless spring,
    One known from all the seraph band
By softer voice, by smile and wing
    More exquisitely bland!
Here let him speed : to-day this hallow'd air
Is fragrant with a mother's first and fondest prayer.

Only let Heaven her fire impart,
    No richer incense breathes on earth :
" A spouse with all a daughter's heart,"
    Fresh from the perilous birth,
To the great Father lifts her pale glad eye,
Like a reviving flower when storms are hush'd on high.

O what a treasure of sweet thought
    Is here ! what hope and joy and love
All in one tender bosom brought,
    For the all-gracious Dove
To brood o'er silently, and form for heaven
Each passionate wish and dream to dear affection given.

Her fluttering heart, too keenly blest,
    Would sicken, but she leans on Thee,
Sees Thee by faith on Mary's breast,
    And breathes serene and free.
Slight tremblings only of her veil declare [m]
Soft answers duly whisper'd to each soothing prayer.

[m] When the woman comes to this office, the rubric, as it was altered
at the last review, directs that she be *decently apparelled,* i.e. as the
custom and order was formerly, *with a white covering* or *veil.*
Wheatley on the Common Prayer, c. xiii. sect. i. 3.

We are too weak, when Thou dost bless,
　To bear the joy—help, Virgin-born !
By thine own mother's first caress,
　That wak'd thy natal morn !
Help, by the unexpressive smile, that made
A heaven on earth around the couch where Thou wast
　laid !

Commination.

THE prayers are o'er : why slumberest thou so
      long,
         Thou voice of sacred song ?
Why swell'st thou not, like breeze from mountain
      cave,
         High o'er the echoing nave,
The white-rob'd priest, as otherwhile, to guide,
         Up to the altar's northern side ?—
   A mourner's tale of shame and sad decay
Keeps back our glorious sacrifice to-day :

   The widow'd Spouse of Christ : with ashes crown'd,
         Her Christmas robes unbound,
   She lingers in the porch for grief and fear,
         Keeping her penance drear.—
   O is it nought to you ? that idly gay,
         Or coldly proud, ye turn away ?
But if her warning tears in vain be spent,
Lo, to her alter'd eye the Law's stern fires are lent.

   Each awful curse, that on Mount Ebal rang,
         Peals with a direr clang
   Out of that silver trump, whose tones of old
         Forgiveness only told.
   And who can blame the mother's fond affright [n],
         Who sporting on some giddy height
   Her infant sees, and springs with hurried hand
To snatch the rover from the dangerous strand ?

[n] Alluding to a beautiful anecdote in the Greek Anthology, tom.
i. 180. ed. Jacobs. See Pleasures of Memory, p. 133.

But surer than all words the silent spell,
  So Grecian legends tell,
When to her bird, too early scap'd the nest,
  She bares her tender breast.
Smiling he turns and spreads his little wing,
  There to glide home, there safely cling.
So yearns our mother o'er each truant son,
So softly falls the lay in fear and wrath begun.

  Wayward and spoil'd she knows ye : the keen blast,
    That brac'd her youth, is past :
  The rod of discipline, the robe of shame—
    She bears them in your name :
  Only return and love.   But ye perchance
    Are deeper plung'd in sorrow's trance :
  Your God forgives, but ye no comfort take
Till ye have scourg'd the sins that in your conscience ache.

  O heavy laden soul ! kneel down and hear
    Thy penance in calm fear :
  With thine own lips to sentence all thy sin ;
    Then, by the judge within
  Absolv'd, in thankful sacrifice to part
    For ever with thy sullen heart,
  Nor on remorseful thoughts to brood, and stain
The glory of the Cross, forgiven and cheer'd in vain.

Forms of Prayer to be used at Sea.

When thou passest through the waters I will be with thee. Isaiah xliii. 2.

THE shower of moonlight falls as still and clear
    Upon the desert main,
As where sweet flowers some pastoral garden cheer
    With fragrance after rain :
The wild winds rustle in the piping shrouds,
    As in the quivering trees :
Like summer fields, beneath the shadowy clouds
    The yielding waters darken in the breeze.

Thou too art here with thy soft inland tones,
    Mother of our new birth ;
The lonely ocean learns thy orisons,
    And loves thy sacred mirth :
When storms are high, or when the fires of war
    Come lightening round our course,
Thou breath'st a note like music from afar,
    Tempering rude hearts with calm angelic force.

Far far away, the homesick seaman's hoard,
    Thy fragrant tokens live,
Like flower-leaves in a precious volume stor'd,
    To solace and relieve
Some heart too weary of the restless world ;
    Or like thy sabbath Cross,
That o'er the brightening billow streams unfurl'd,
    Whatever gale the labouring vessel toss.

O kindly soothing in high Victory's hour,
    Or when a comrade dies,

In whose sweet presence Sorrow dares not lower,
      Nor Expectation rise
Too high for earth ; what mother's heart could spare
      To the cold cheerless deep
Her flower and hope ? but thou art with him there,
      Pledge of the untir'd arm and eye that cannot sleep :

The eye that watches o'er wild Ocean's dead,
      Each in his coral cave,
Fondly as if the green turf wrapt his head
      Fast by his father's grave.—
One moment, and the seeds of life shall spring
      Out of the waste abyss,
And happy warriors triumph with their King
      In worlds without a sea °, unchanging orbs of bliss.

° And there was no more sea. *Revelation* xxi. 1.

19

Gunpowder Treason.

As thou hast testified of me in Jerusalem, so must thou bear witness also at Rome. Acts xxiii. 11.

BENEATH the burning eastern sky
    The Cross was rais'd at morn :
The widow'd Church to weep stood by,
    The world, to hate and scorn.

Now, journeying westward, evermore
    We know the lonely Spouse
By the dear mark her Saviour bore
    Trac'd on her patient brows.

At Rome she wears it, as of old
    Upon th' accursed hill :
By monarchs clad in gems and gold,
    She goes a mourner still.

She mourns that tender hearts should bend
    Before a meaner shrine,
And upon Saint or Angel spend
    The love that should be thine.

By day and night her sorrows fall
    Where miscreant hands and rude
Have stain'd her pure ethereal pall
    With many a martyr's blood.

And yearns not her parental heart,
    To hear *their* secret sighs,
Upon whose doubting way apart
    Bewildering shadows rise ?

Who to her side in peace would cling,
But fear to wake, and find
What they had deem'd her genial wing
Was Error's soothing blind.

She treasures up each throbbing prayer :
Come, trembler, come and pour
Into her bosom all thy care,
For she has balm in store.

Her gentle teaching sweetly blends
With the clear light of Truth
Th' aerial gleam that Fancy lends
To solemn thoughts in youth.—

If thou hast lov'd, in hours of gloom,
To dream the dead are near,
And people all the lonely room
With guardian spirits dear,

Dream on the soothing dream at will :
The lurid mist is o'er,
That shew'd the righteous suffering still
Upon th' eternal shore.

If with thy heart the strains accord,
That on His altar-throne
Highest exalt thy glorious Lord,
Yet leave Him most thine own ;

O come to our Communion Feast :
There present in the heart,
Not in the hands, th' eternal Priest
Will his true self impart.—

Thus, should thy soul misgiving turn
Back to th' enchanted air,

Solace and warning thou mayst learn
    From all that tempts thee there.

And O ! by all the pangs and fears
    Fraternal spirits know,
When for an elder's shame the tears
    Of wakeful anguish flow,

Speak gently of our sister's fall :
    Who knows but gentle love
May win her at our patient call
    The surer way to prove?

King Charles the Martyr.

This is thankworthy, if a man for conscience toward God endure grief, suffering wrongfully. 1 St. Peter ii. 19.

PRAISE to our pardoning God ! though silent now
    The thunders of the deep prophetic sky,
Though in our sight no powers of darkness bow
    Before th' Apostles' glorious company ;

The Martyrs' noble army still is ours,
    Far in the North our fallen days have seen
How in her woe the tenderest spirit towers,
    For Jesus' sake in agony serene.

Praise to our God ! not cottage hearths alone,
    And shades impervious to the proud world's glare,
Such witness yield : a monarch from his throne
    Springs to his Cross and finds his glory there.

Yes : wheresoe'er one trace of thee is found,
    As in the Sacred Land, the shadows fall :
With beating hearts we roam the haunted ground,
    Lone battle field, or crumbling prison hall.

And there are aching solitary breasts,
    Whose widow'd walk with thought of thee is cheer'd,
Our own, our royal Saint : thy memory rests
    On many a prayer, the more for thee endear'd.

True son of our dear Mother, early taught
    With her to worship and for her to die,
Nurs'd in her aisles to more than kingly thought,
    Oft in her solemn hours we dream thee nigh.

For thou didst love to trace her daily lore,
　And where we look for comfort or for calm,
Over the self-same lines to bend, and pour
　Thy heart with hers in some victorious psalm.

And well did she thy loyal love repay ;
　When all forsook, her Angels still were nigh,
Chain'd and bereft, and on thy funeral way,
　Straight to the Cross she turn'd thy dying eye P.

And yearly now, before the Martyrs' King,
　For thee she offers her maternal tears,
Calls us, like thee, to His dear feet to cling,
　And bury in His wounds our earthly fears.

The Angels hear, and there is mirth in Heaven,
　Fit prelude of the joy, when spirits won
Like thee to patient Faith, shall rise forgiven,
　And at their Saviour's knees thy bright example own.

P " His Majesty then bade him, Mr. Herbert, withdraw ; for he
was about an hour in private with the Bishop (Juxon) : and being
called in, the Bishop went to prayer ; and reading also the 27th
chapter of the Gospel of St. Matthew, which relateth the Passion of
our Blessed Saviour. The King, after the Service was done, asked
the Bishop, if he had made choice of that chapter, being so appli-
cable to his present condition ? The Bishop replied, ' May it please
your Gracious Majesty, it is the proper lesson for the day, as appears
by the Kalendar ;' which the King was much affected with, so aptly
serving as a seasonable preparation for his death that day."
Herbert's Memoirs, p. 131.

The Restoration of the Royal Family.

And Barzillai said unto the king, How long have I to live, that I should go up with the king unto Jerusalem? 2 Samuel xix. 34.

AS when the Paschal week is o'er,
    Sleeps in the silent aisles no more
        The breath of sacred song,
But by the rising Saviour's light
Awaken'd soars in airy flight,
        Or deepening rolls along ¶;

The while round altar, niche, and shrine,
The funeral evergreens entwine,
        And a dark brilliance cast,
The brighter for their hues of gloom,
Tokens of Him, who through the tomb
        Into high glory pass'd :

Such were the lights and such the strains,
When proudly stream'd o'er Ocean plains
        Our own returning Cross ;
For with that triumph seem'd to float
Far on the breeze one dirgelike note
        Of orphanhood and loss.

Father and King, O where art thou ?
A greener wreath adorns thy brow,
        And clearer rays surround ;
O for one hour of prayer like thine,

¶ The organ is silent in many Churches during Passion week : and in some it is the custom to put up evergreen boughs at Easter as well as at Christmas time.

To plead before th' all-ruling shrine
    For Britain lost and found !

And he [r], whose mild persuasive voice
Taught us in trials to rejoice,
    Most like a faithful Dove,
That by some ruin'd homestead builds,
And pours to the forsaken fields
    His wonted lay of love :

Why comes he not to bear his part,
To lift and guide th' exulting heart ?—
    A hand that cannot spare
Lies heavy on his gentle breast :
We wish him health ; he sighs for rest,
    And Heaven accepts the prayer.

Yes, go in peace, dear placid spright,
Ill spar'd ; but would we store aright
    Thy serious sweet farewell,
We need not grudge thee to the skies,
Sure after thee in time to rise,
    With thee for ever dwell.

Till then, whene'er with duteous hand,
Year after year, my native Land
    Her royal offering brings,
Upon the Altar lays the Crown,
And spreads her robes of old renown
    Before the King of Kings,

Be some kind spirit, likest thine,
Ever at hand, with airs divine
    The wandering heart to seize ;
Whispering, " How long hast thou to live,
" That thou shouldst Hope or Fancy give
    " To flowers or crowns like these ? "

[r] Read Fell's Life of Hammond, p. 283—296. Oxford, 1806.

The Accession.

As I was with Moses, so I will be with thee : I will not fail thee, nor forsake thee. Joshua i. 5.

THE voice that from the glory came
    To tell how Moses died unseen,
And waken Joshua's spear of flame
    To victory on the mountains green,
Its trumpet tones are sounding still,
    ˙ When Kings or Parents pass away,
They greet us with a cheering thrill
    Of power and comfort in decay.

Behind the soft bright summer cloud
    That makes such haste to melt and die,
Our wistful gaze is oft allow'd
    A glimpse of the unchanging sky :
Let storm and darkness do their worst ;
    For the lost dream the heart may ache,
The heart may ache, but may not burst :
    Heaven will not leave thee nor forsake.

One rock amid the weltering floods,
    One torch in a tempestuous night,
One changeless pine in fading woods :—
    Such is the thought of Love and Might,
True Might and ever-present Love,
    When Death is busy near the throne,
And Sorrow her keen sting would prove
    On Monarchs orphan'd and alone.

In that lorn hour and desolate,
    Who could endure a crown ? but He,

Who singly bore the world's sad weight,
　Is near, to whisper, " Lean on me :
" Thy days of toil, thy nights of care,
　" Sad lonely dreams in crowded hall,
" Darkness within, while pageants glare
　" Around—the Cross supports them all."

O Promise of undying Love !
　While Monarchs seek thee for repose,
Far in the nameless mountain cove
　Each pastoral heart thy bounty knows.
Ye, who in place of shepherds true
　Come trembling to their awful trust,
Lo here the fountain to imbue
　With strength and hope your feeble dust.

Not upon Kings or Priests alone
　The power of that dear word is spent ;
It chants to all in softest tone
　The lowly lesson of Content :
Heaven's light is pour'd on high and low ;
　To high and low Heaven's Angel spake ;
" Resign thee to thy weal or woe,
　" I ne'er will leave thee nor forsake."

Ordination.

After this, the Congregation shall be desired secretly in their prayers to make their humble supplications to God for all these things : for the which prayers there shall be silence kept for a space.

After which shall be sung or said by the Bishop, the persons to be ordained Priests all kneeling, " Veni, Creator Spiritus." Rubric in the Office for Ordering of Priests.

'TWAS silence in thy temple, Lord,
    When slowly through the hallow'd air
The spreading cloud of incense soar'd,
    Charg'd with the breath of Israel's prayer.

'Twas silence round thy throne on high,
    When the last wondrous seal unclos'd [s],
And in the portals of the sky
    Thine armies awfully repos'd.

And this deep pause, that o'er us now
    Is hovering—comes it not of Thee?
Is it not like a Mother's vow,
    When with her darling on her knee,

She weighs and numbers o'er and o'er
    Love's treasure hid in her fond breast,
To cull from that exhaustless store
    The dearest blessing and the best?

[s] When he had opened the seventh seal, there was silence in heaven about the space of half an hour. *Rev.* viii. 1.

And where shall Mother's bosom find,
    With all its deep love-learned skill,
A prayer so sweetly to her mind,
    As, in this sacred hour and still,

Is wafted from the white-rob'd choir,
    Ere yet the pure high-breathed lay,
" Come, Holy Ghost, our souls inspire,"
    Rise floating on its dove-like way.

And when it comes, so deep and clear
    The strain, so soft the melting fall,
It seems not to th' entranced ear
    Less than thine own heart-cheering call,

Spirit of Christ—thine earnest given
    That these our prayers are heard, and they,
Who grasp, this hour, the sword of Heaven,
    Shall feel thee on their weary way.

Oft as at morn or soothing eve
    Over the Holy Fount they lean,
Their fading garland freshly weave,
    Or fan them with thine airs serene,

Spirit of Light and Truth ! to Thee
    We trust them in that musing hour,
Till they, with open heart and free,
    Teach all Thy word in all its power.

When foemen watch their tents by night,
    And mists hang wide o'er moor and fell,
Spirit of Counsel and of Might,
    Their pastoral warfare guide Thou well.

And O ! when worn and tir'd they sigh
    With that more fearful war within,
When Passion's storms are loud and high,
    And brooding o'er remember'd sin

The heart dies down—O mightiest then,
Come ever true, come ever near,
And wake their slumbering love again,
Spirit of God's most holy Fear!

INDEX.

	PAGE
AND is there in God's world so drear a place	66
And wilt Thou hear the fever'd heart	32
Angel of wrath ! why linger in mid air	64
As rays around the source of light	20
As when the Paschal week is o'er	279
At length the worst is o'er, and Thou art laid	91
Awake—again the Gospel-trump is blown	6
BENEATH the burning eastern sky	274
Bless'd are the pure in heart	212
CREATOR, Saviour, strengthening Guide	131
DEAR is the morning gale of spring	222
FATHER to me Thou art and Mother dear	79
Fill high the bowl, and spice it well, and pour	82
First Father of the holy seed	103
Foe of mankind ! too bold thy race	56
Go not away, thou weary soul	151
Go up and watch the new born rill	97

	PAGE
HOLD up thy mirror to the sun	235
Hues of the rich unfolding morn	1
I MARK'D a rainbow in the north	43
In troublous days of anguish and rebuke	155
Is it not strange, the darkest hour	89
Is there, in bowers of endless spring	268
Is this a time to plant and build	160
It is so—ope thine eyes, and see	178
It was not then a poet's dream	141
LESSONS sweet of spring returning	38
Lord, and what shall this man do	22
Lord, in thy field I work all day	128
MY Saviour, can it ever be	111
NOT till the freezing blast is still	9
Now is there solemn pause in earth and heaven	114
O FOR a sculptor's hand	106
O God of Mercy, God of Might	252
O hateful spell of Sin! when friends are nigh	139
O holy mountain of my God	87
O Lord my God, do Thou thy holy will	84
O Thou who deign'st to sympathize	217
O Youth and Joy, your airy tread	263
Of the bright things in earth and air	14
Oh! day of days! shall hearts set free	94
Oh! say not, dream not, heavenly notes	257

	PAGE
Oh ! who shall dare in this frail scene	220
On Sinai's top, in prayer and trance .	165
PRAISE to our pardoning God ! though silent now	277
Prophet of God, arise and take .	153
RED o'er the forest peers the setting sun .	191
SAY, ye celestial guards, who wait	24
See Lucifer like lightning fall .	69
Seest thou, how tearful and alone	248
Since all that is not heaven must fade	124
Sit down and take thy fill of joy	233
Soft cloud, that while the breeze of May .	117
Star of the East, how sweet art Thou	35
Stately thy walls, and holy are the prayers	175
Sweet dove ! the softest, steadiest plume .	59
Sweet nurslings of the vernal skies .	171
TEN cleans'd and only one remain .	169
'Tis gone, that bright and orbed blaze	4
'Tis true, of old th' unchanging sun .	25
The bright-hair'd morn is glowing	197
The clouds that wrap the setting sun	136
The earth that in her genial breast .	119
The heart of childhood is all mirth .	40
Th' historic Muse, from age to age .	74
The live-long night we've toil'd in vain	145
The midday sun, with fiercest glare .	208
The morning mist is cleared away	187

20

	PAGE
The prayers are o'er : why slumberest thou so long . . .	270
The shadow of th' Almighty's cloud	259
The shower of moonlight falls as still and clear	272
The Son of God in doing good	162
The voice that from the glory came	281
The world's a room of sickness, where each heart . . .	224
The year begins with Thee	29
There are, who darkling and alone	51
There is an awe in mortals' joy	261
There is a book, who runs may read	54
They know th' Almighty's power	46
Thou first-born of the year's delight	100
Thou thrice denied, yet thrice belov'd	230
'Twas silence in thy temple, Lord	283
Twice in her season of decay	227
Two clouds before the summer gale	244
WAKE, arm divine ! awake	48
We were not by when Jesus came	205
Well may I guess and feel	109
What liberty so glad and gay	189
What sudden blaze of song	17
What went ye out to see	11
When bitter thoughts, of conscience born	148
When brothers part for manhood's race	203
When God of old came down from heaven	122
When Nature tries her finest touch	71
When Persecution's torrent blaze	182
Where is it mothers learn their love	255

	PAGE
Where is the land with milk and honey flowing	134
Where is thy favour'd haunt, eternal Voice	185
Who is God's chosen priest	215
Who says, the wan autumnal sun	265
Why blow'st thou not, thou wintry wind	250
Why doth my Saviour weep	158
Why should we faint and fear to live alone	194
Will God indeed with fragments bear	200
Wish not, dear friends, my pain away	173
Ye hermits blest, ye holy maids	238
Ye stars that round the Sun of righteousness	241
Ye whose hearts are beating high	77
Yes—deep within and deeper yet	62

THE END.